Selected Poems Rogha Dánta

MÁIRTÍN Ó DIREÁIN

Selected Poems

MÁIRTÍN Ó DIREÁIN

Rogha Dánta

EDITED AND TRANSLATED BY FRANK SEWELL

WAKE
FOREST
UNIVERSITY
PRESS

First North American edition

First published by Cló Iar-Chonnacht,
An Spidéal, Co. na Gaillimhe/Galway, Ireland

For permission, write to
Wake Forest University Press
Post Office Box 7333
Winston-Salem, NC 27109
WFUPRESS.WFU.EDU
WFUPRESS@WFU.EDU

ISBN 978-1-930630-90-1 (paperback)
LCCN 2019944718

Designed and typeset by
Nathan W. Moehlmann,
Goosepen Studio & Press

Publication of this book was generously
supported by the Boyle Family Fund.

Clár / Contents

---

from Ó *Mórna* (1957)

---

from Ár *Ré Dhearóil* [Our Wretched Era] (1962)

---

from *Cloch Choirnéil* [Cornerstone] (1966)

from *Crainn is Cairde* [Trees and Friends] (1970)

---

from *Ceacht an Éin* [The Bird's Lesson] (1979)

Dánta Eile / Other Poems (uncollected, 1951–1979)

RÉAMHRÁ

sliocht as Do Mo Dhánta

Faighidís caidéis díbh
Na comharsain, más áil leo é,
Tá sibh gléasta agam,
Go feadh m'acmhainne féin,
Gan cabhair ó aon,
Is bíodh a fhios acu feasta
Nár tháinig ní gan cháim
Ach ó láimh Dé.

Cá bhfuil an t-aiteas
Trínar lingeadh sibh,
I gcéaduair ar an saol?
Is tá inchis bhur dtoirchithe
Imithe mar thinneas ó aréir,
Ach mo bheannacht in bhur dteannta
Ós mé bhur n-athair go léir...

FOREWORD

from To My Poems

Neighbors may pass remarks
About you all they like,
But I have fitted you out
As best I can,
With help from no one;
And they should know from now
That perfection only comes
From the hand of God.

Where is the thrill
With which you leapt
At first into this life?
The trouble over your delivery
Is like a forgotten illness;
But as I'm father to you all,
I bless you on your way...

INTRODUCTION

A KING OF WORDS[1]: MÁIRTÍN Ó DIREÁIN

Máirtín Ó Direáin (1910–88), in his poem "Ionracas" ["Integrity"] from his 1957 collection *Ó Mórna*, agreed with critic and fellow poet Seán Ó Ríordáin (whom Ó Direáin considered a literary "brother") that the subjects and *raisons d'être* of his poetry were "an island and a woman's love."[2] Ó Direáin's work covers more than just two themes but even if it were characterized by any one of the two themes mentioned by Ó Ríordáin, his treatment of that theme would still manage to be plural and multidimensional. For example, the island (his home island of Inis Mór, the largest of the three Aran Islands) is represented in Ó Direáin's work in a variety of forms. In the early poem "Faoiseamh a Gheobhadsa" ["Peace"] (1942), the island offers a very temporary "respite" from the madding crowd of modern city life; and shortly later, in "An tEarrach Thiar" ["Springtime in the West"] (1949), it supplies a gilded gallery of visual and aural images or comforting memories—fragments to shore against the ruins of modern city (and mostly Galltacht[3]) life. However, from the same 1949 collection, *Rogha Dánta* [*Selected Poems*], Ó Direáin also provides a more nuanced and realistic portrait of his "oileán rún" [beloved island] in poems such as "Árainn 1947" in which a string of treasured images is again recounted but, this time, ruefully declared to be absent from the poet's (and, in his view, from the island's) present, having slipped into the past:

> Ní don óige feasta
> An sceirdoileán cúng úd.
>
> [Not for the young anymore,
> That narrow, wind-scoured island.]

The latter viewpoint is repeated in Ó Direáin's next major collection, *Ó Mórna* (1957), which laments the end of his own era[4] on the island (which he had left almost thirty years earlier) and which goes as far as predicting the end of the island itself, which the poet foresees as becoming abandoned before it finally sinks beneath the waves.[5] By 1966, Ó Direáin records his own painful sense of being a "stranger" on his home island when he returns to visit;[6] and, in "Berkeley" from the collection *Cloch Choirnéil* [*Cornerstone*] of the same year, he acknowledges that the island (with its "grey stones [...] turning into dreams in my mind"[7]) has become, for him, less a reality and more a metaphor, a semi-remembered, a semi-imagined place. Seamus Heaney wrote "my last things will be first things slipping from me,"[8] a line which is equally true of Ó Direáin, one of whose last poems about his beloved or, latterly, secret island[9] raised the following question:

> Sleamhnaíonn nithe neamhbheo
> Siar ón mbeo go bhfágann é:
> An amhlaidh sin a d'fhág
> An t-oileán mo dhán,
> Nó ar thugais faoi deara é?[10]
>
> [Unliving things slip away
> From life until they leave it:
> Is that how the island left
> My poem? Or did you notice?]

Thus, although the island (his motherland and place of origin) remained a constant touchstone and theme for Ó Direáin, it turned out to be "incorrigibly plural"[11] in terms of its representation in his work. Consequently, the reader is left to wonder if the poet's real subject (in such poems) is the island and its rich culture or, rather, memory which itself is paradoxically both a comfort ("a feather in the pillow"[12]) and salt in the wound[13] of separation and loss.

The second theme noted by Ó Ríordáin, and again acknowledged by Ó Direáin, was "a woman's love"—but which woman and what kind of relationship? It is evident from the poems that an early love affair and broken relationship haunts many of Ó Direáin's poems,[14] even if he remains circumspect about the identity of the particular Aran-island Beatrice dei Bardi[15] or Maud Gonne who set him off on the well-worn poets' path of longing for an absent Muse:

Nuair a luaitear d'ainm liom,
  A bhean nach luaifead féin,
Ní osclaímse mo bhéal
  Ach déanaim gáire beag.

[Whenever they say your name to me,
Woman I will not mention,
I don't let slip a single word,
But smile just a fraction.][16]

As with his island memories, recollections of lost love sometimes provoke more pain than pleasure:

Caoin tú féin anois, a bhean!
Cé mall an gol sin agat,
Fadó a chaoin mise thú,
Níl deoir eile agam.[17]

[Cry for yourself now, woman,
Although you left it late;
I cried for you long ago
And have no more tears to shed.]

Elsewhere a woman's love prompts Pushkin-like[18] resignation:

Más caolsnáth caite an gad,
Tú féin do spíon é amhlaidh,
Dual ar dhual do spíonais é;
Ar fhigh tú ó shin a shamhail?[19]

[If the (love-)knot is threadbare,
You have made it so.
Strand by strand you stripped it;
Did you weave its like again?]

Occasionally, and in consciously traditional fashion, romantic love is presented as a battle of the sexes with female beauty imaged as a weapon, and inconstancy as a dagger, leaving the poet, once again, with the wound of loss which prompts his poetry: see, for example, "An Ghoin" ["The Wound"].[20] At other times, however, the woman is a victim of her own mutability, poisoned or corrupted by a false male tempter:

Rinne cloch de do chroí íogair
Nuair a chuir i do chluais an fríd
A chuir cor i leamhnacht na beatha ort,
A rinne meadhg de do shaol.[21]

[He turned your tender heart to stone
When he put in your ear the mite
That turned your sweet life-milk sour
And curdled away your life.]

Yet, women in Ó Direáin's poetry are not confined to being represented solely as love objects whether faithful or unfaithful. In addition, women of the poet's acquaintance are frequently celebrated or commemorated in poems for individuals, including Pegg Monahan,[22] a friend whom Ó Direáin praises for her discernment and humor; the actress Máire Nic Giolla Mhártain whom he eulogizes for bringing to life on stage literary heroines such as Deirdre and Siobhán;[23] his own mother whose fortitude and forbearance in the face of poverty and grief he acknowledges in numerous poems;[24] his wife Áine Colivet whom the poet loved and mourned in poems such as "Fuacht is Faitíos" ["Cold Fear"] and "Tuige Duit a Theacht?" ["Why Do You Come Here?"];[25] and women artists such as the poet

Caitlín Maude and singer Treasa Ní Mhiolláin whose transformative creative powers he numbers in his song.[26]

Undeniably, however, some women or, rather, types of women are castigated in particular poems: for example, the allegedly materialistic, half-hearted and uncommitted women of "Ár Ré Dhearóil" ["Our Wretched Era"] who (in Ó Direáin's depiction) deem it fashionable and, therefore, worthwhile to travel abroad and briefly dabble in foreign languages while, presumably, they would balk at the idea of engaging more deeply (or at all) with their own country's culture and language—a post-colonial, skewed mentality that Nuala Ní Dhomhnaill has also critically commented upon.[27] There is something objectionable and too much "of its time"[28] about Ó Direáin's view (in the same poem) that such women would be better rewarded by pregnancy and motherhood, but his critique of modern, urban people of both genders in this poem is of a piece with his general dislike of apparent selfishness, shallow fashion-following and wealth-seeking. Ó Direáin sharply contrasts these latter with selfless devotion of the kind demonstrated by, for example, deeply committed artists (such as Sean O'Casey, Eoghan Ó Tuairisc and Caitlín Maude) and even more committed political figures (such as the socialist James Connolly and internationalist Patrick Pearse). Notable, in this context, is Ó Direáin's panegyric of "Mná na hAiséirí" ["The Women of the (Easter) Rising"]:

Nuair a tháinig thar toinn anall na hamhais,
Nuair a chuaigh clann na saoirse leo chun catha
Bhí an bhuíon arís gan scíth sa mbearna
Ar fiannas i bhfochair na bhfianna calma
Ina gcranna fortaigh ag clann na gaile.[29]

[When mercenary thugs[30] came over the sea
And freedom fighters went to war with them,
That band of women were tireless in defense,
Serving alongside our brave warriors,
Pillars of support to that clan of heroes.]

Ó Direáin was one of the extremely few Irish poets to eulogize the contribution of Cumann na mBan and other women's organizations in the struggle for Irish independence. For example, as recently as 2016 during the centenary celebrations of the Easter Rising it was still commonly claimed that no Irish *male* poet had honored the heroines of 1916 when Ó Direáin had clearly done so in this (admittedly neglected) poem from, arguably, his most famous collection, *Ó Mórna* (1957).

Indeed, of the two themes highlighted by Ó Ríordáin and acknowledged by Ó Direáin, most critical emphasis by far has been given to the island and an insufficient amount of attention has been paid to Ó Direáin's "second" theme: women. The latter actually frame his complete poetic oeuvre, lighting the candles of memory that sparked his first poems,[31] and taking the spotlight of the final poem in his very last collection:

Misneach uile mná ár dtíre
Ach ar ghualainn Ghráinne an Iarthair
Ní raibh i nGráinne Fhinn
Ach áilleagán mná is peata:
Samhaill Mháire Rua í Gráinne Ní Mháille
Nó b'fhéidir Méabh Chruachan.[32]

[Our country's women
Are made of courage,
But next to Gráinne Mhaol,[33]
Finn McCool's Gráinne
Is a dolly bird, a pet;
Our "Grace-of-the-West"
Is more akin to Red Mary[34]
or else, perhaps, Medbh
of Croghan, Queen of Connacht.]

An argument could easily be made that women are far more important in Ó Direáin's work than has been appreciated to date, especially if one adds the female or feminine presence within the male psyche, including that of the poet—a topic or theme which he explores with acute anxiety typical of the period in which he was writing.

In common with poets writing in English during the mid-to-late twentieth century, Ó Direáin often demonstrates strict binary thinking about masculinity: in "Na Coillteáin" ["The Eunuchs"],[35] critics of his poetry are depicted as lacking in masculinity and, therefore, envying the man or poet with "stones," signifying "balls." Elsewhere, at times, being a writer (especially a writer, like himself, of clerical files in a modern city office) is itself presented by Ó Direáin as a sign of diminished masculinity and even fertility: the "uprooted" or deracinated urban Irish citizens of "Stoite" ["Uprooted"] will not be remembered for the house or dry stone wall they build and leave behind, but for "A pile of papers / Buried in dust, / Left behind / In a Govt. office."[36] Similarly, in "Gleic Mo Dhaoine" ["My People's Struggle"] a clear contrast is drawn between Aran-island manly wrestling against rock and ocean versus the "slyness," "shallow tricks" and "superior" notions of class distinction which Ó Direáin associates with city life.[37] Cut off or "uprooted" from nature and native culture, ageing,[38] the very nation's own candle burning out,[39] Ó Direáin briefly (and ruefully) seeks, at one point, a solution in wishing for some great male savior figure to rescue Ireland and its culture but mostly he turns (as both a private citizen and a poet) to "learning" and to literature,[40] even though he does not always view those as the most manly of pursuits.

Wonder at the world and the spoken word was, however, a lifelong habit or state of being for Ó Direáin.[41] As a youth he appeared to his neighbors to be a dreamer but was, in fact, an artist, absorbing his surroundings and storing lasting sense-impressions that would fuel the fire of his creativity for as long as it would stay lit. He started off, on Aran, building rock sculptures of island people and later moved towards poetry, a form of word sculpture. In a life of art, he found that, sometimes, "the craft" could provide "solace"[42] but, paradoxically, art was also a "burden," creating a divided self and leading to a spiritual conflict between pride and humility, a lonely road even if it was previously trod by Aogán Ó Rathaille and others.[43] Moreover, one could never be sure of staying in Pegasus' saddle or of always landing a catch or a poem.[44]

Upon leaving Aran at the age of eighteen, Ó Direáin went to Galway where he was active in the Gaelic League and in An Taibhdhearc,[45] reading and performing in plays, and even writing a play about early twentieth-century Russian poet Alexander Blok—a sign of his international interests and tastes, favoring authors who lived through, and examined, changing times during, or after, upheavals such as revolution and war. His reading over the years included works by mainland European philosophers (such as Nietzsche, Berdyaev, and Spengler) as well as literature by favorites such as T. S. Eliot (from whose poems and essays he would quote at will, in English, including while delivering talks in Irish), Sean O'Casey and W. B. Yeats, as well as Irish-language authors past and present. From his many eulogies and/or elegies to writers, and from his comments about them, we see that what interested and impressed Ó Direáin most about such writers (in various languages) was their independence, resilience and dedication to the craft, as long as these were combined with one key quality: "daonnacht" [humanity or empathy with others].[46] Their examples, along with his own curiosity and compulsion to write,[47] seem to have kept Ó Direáin going, including through bouts of cultural despair (to which he was prone)[48] and the personal losses charted in his poetry over the years. While he worried intermittently about the power of his medium to survive, mostly he seems to have kept faith that both his own language and the language of poetry still had "the power and substance" (or even the strength of a tiger)[49] for producing biting satire where and when it was needed;[50] and for defending or praising worthy subjects.

In 2018, thirty years after his death, an exhibition entitled "Máirtín Ó Direáin: Fathach File[51] / Reluctant Modernist" (curated by Síobhra Aiken) was held at NUI Galway to commemorate the poet. The designation "reluctant modernist" points to, arguably, Ó Direáin's most important theme: the conflict and contradictions (for individuals and nations) that derive from the exchange between tradition and modernity. Clearly, in some ways, the poet was a traditionalist: for example, he was a native Irish speaker and promoter of the language; even long after leaving Aran, he frequently favored rural values over modern city modes of living, measuring the latter by the yardstick of his early experiences on Aran; and in politics, he was (unsurprisingly) an anti-imperialist internationalist. But what this means is that, in practice, he was open to receiving art and ideas both from his own culture (past and present) and also from a wide range of languages and cultures. In "Solas" ["Light"], he explains:

Ariamh níor dhiúltaigh solas
Ó na ceithre hairde nuair tháinig;
Ach iarraim ar an solas iasachta
Gan mo sholas féin a mhúchadh.[52]

[I never rejected light
From anywhere when it came;
But I ask the foreign light
Not to drown out my own.]

Thus, while he was interested in preserving and continuing Irish-language culture (including poetry), he was also willing to extend tradition by incorporating elements from outside the tradition. If, for example, in poetry he found that the old forms were dead or done to near-death,[53] then part of the solution for Ó Direáin (as for Seamus Heaney) was to "learn from Eliot"[54] and other writers to forge freer poetic lines based on patterns of speech rather than always (or too inflexibly) on the "fixed" forms and strict meter of earlier poetry. Doing so enabled Ó Direáin to become, in Cathal Ó Searcaigh's terms, a "fuascailteoir" ["liberator"] of words, freeing them from the "prison of oblivion"[55] and setting them to use in poetry, where readers ever since (including subsequent generations of poets such as Nuala Ní Dhomhnaill, Celia de Fréine, Pól Ó Muirí and Gearóid Mac Lochlainn) could savor and wonder at them, their sound, sense, memorability and quotability.

Ó Direáin's reluctant modernism is also in evidence in his poems that focus on (another main theme) the city, usually Dublin in his case. In most of his city-based poems, he is distrustful of the urban milieu, its fast-changing fashions and movement, its crowded streets where vast numbers of people are herded together like "prisoners"[56] or even "ants"[57] and where tradition or "custom" can quickly become outmoded or rejected; however, Ó Direáin himself came to artistic life in the city of Galway (once renowned throughout Europe, he tells us in "Ceannaithe" ["Merchants"][58]) and he seems to have enjoyed (to an extent) the Gaelic and general cultural scene and literary camaraderie of Dublin,[59] where he lived for most of his life. Most significantly, there is one poem in which, like Louis MacNeice, Ó Direáin acknowledges that there is "beauty [...] in this vast organism grown out of us,"[60] the city:

Caithimse sealta in éad
Leis an dream a d'fhás
I dtaithí áilleacht chathartha,
Eaglais, stua, is foirgneamh ard [...].[61]

[There are times I'm jealous
Of the crowd that grew up
Familiar with urban beauty,
Cathedral, arch, tall building...]

Published in the magazine *Feasta* as far back as 1951, this poem is, however, so uncharacteristic of Ó Direáin's usually negative depiction of the city that it was not gathered into any individual collection by the poet: it was only finally rounded up, in 1980, in his collected poems up to that point: *Dánta 1939–1979*.[62] The poem concludes with the statement that "first things" (Aran-island culture) retain first place in his affections, however, the admission of "jealousy" in this context significantly problematizes the unflattering portrayal of city life elsewhere in his work. But both his living through and writing about these and other contradictions that spring from the "uprootedness" experienced by generations of Irish people, contribute to the enduring fascination of Ó Direáin's work.

Moreover, his themes and concerns are not merely, or uniquely, Irish ones. Ó Direáin was interested in Nietzschean ideas such as the "will to power," as exhibited, for example, by that hard-riding country gentleman Ó Mórna, in the poem by that name.[63] Ó Mórna's will or desire to live, procreate, and go beyond bounds of morality, etc., make him a creature of fascination for Ó Direáin, an embodiment of patriarchal power gone wild, even toxic. Ó Mórna's individual rise and fall seem to mirror that of nations, empires and possibly even cultures in general. Ó Direáin had certainly been reading Oswald Spengler's *The Decline of the West* in which cultures are viewed as superorganisms with a limited and predictable lifespan. Such ideas, Ó Direáin said, "set his thoughts dancing" or, at least, wondering if Spengler's notion of the morphology of culture would explain not only the decline of cultures such as the Babylonian and Egyptian (among Spengler's interests) but also the rise and so-called "collapse" (actual destruction) of the Gaelic order, the slow decline of the English empire, the fall of the Ascendancy and the possible drowning out of Gaelic culture (among others):

An lá a bhfuil srathair is diallait
Faoi iamh sa mhúsaem
Cá mór nach ionann ár gcás?[64]

[The day when yoke and saddle
Are locked up in a museum,
Won't our position be the same?]

The words "deireadh" [end] and "bás" [death], together with related images and ideas, are frequent in Ó Direáin's poetry. With the early death of his father and brother, he was accustomed to loss from an early age; and writing in a minority language, often diagnosed as "dying," he was acutely aware of "time's winged chariot hurrying near"[65] for the individual, for any given era and, potentially, for a culture. But there is as much eulogy as elegy in his poetry, as much championing of the underdog as satire of the high and mighty,[66] as much celebration of love as sorrow at its loss. The artist may not always come out on top[67] or "get out of this world alive,"[68] but art does. Ó Direáin's poems transcend time: memories that he so often bore across in memorable lines of poetry are now themselves remembered and quoted by heart where any two Irish-language poets meet, or any student of Irish sits a literature exam. His craft made the poor boy from Aran,[69] the left-leaning republican,[70] a *literary* "king":

> Cén dochar an bás i dtráth?
> Ná maireadh ach dán amháin
> Nó líne a d'aoibhneodh cách
> Beirse i do rí ar oileán.[71]
>
> [What matter death when it comes?
> If one of your poems still stands,
> Or a line that pleases everyone,
> You'll be a king on an island.]

Selected Poems Rogha Dánta

Máirtín Ó Direáin

from

COINNLE GEALA

[Bright Candles]

(1942)

Coinnle ar Lasadh

In oileán beag i gcéin san Iarthar
Beidh coinnle ar lasadh anocht,
I dtithe ceann tuí, is i dtithe ceann slinne,
Dhá cheann déag de choinnle geala a bheas ar lasadh anocht.

Mo chaoinbheannacht siar leis na coinnle geala
A bheas ar lasadh anocht,
Is céad beannacht faoi dhó
Le láimh amháin a lasfas coinnle anocht.

(*Oíche Chinn an Dá Lá Dhéag*, 1939)

Candles Lit

In a little island away in the West
There will be candles lit tonight;
In thatched and in slate-roofed houses,
Twelve bright candles lit tonight.

I send a tender blessing west
To the bright candles lit tonight,
And twice a hundred times I bless
One hand lighting candles tonight.

(*Twelfth Night of Christmas, 1939*)

Do Mhnaoi nach Luaifead

Nuair a luaitear d'ainm liom,
  A bhean nach luaifead féin,
Ní osclaímse mo bhéal
  Ach déanaim gáire beag.

Ní osclaímse mo bhéal
  Ar eagla mo rún a scéitheadh,
Rún nach eol dóibh siúd
  A luann d'ainm liom.

Lionndubh a bhíos os cionn
  An gháire sin a ním,
Ach bród a bhíos ina dháil
  Faoin aithne a chuireas ort.

Faoin aithne a chuireas ort,
  Faoin gcomhrá béil is suilt,
Ní osclaímse mo bhéal,
  A bhean nach luaifead féin.

To X

Whenever they say your name to me,
Woman I will not mention,
I don't let slip a single word,
But smile just a fraction.

I do not say a single word
In case my secret is revealed,
A secret unbeknownst to those
Who mention your name to me.

Black sorrow used to hover over
That secret smile of mine,
But knowing you the way I did,
The sorrow was mixed with pride.

Of knowing you the way I did,
Our joy and conversation,
I don't let slip a single word,
Woman I will not mention.

Faoiseamh a Gheobhadsa

Faoiseamh a gheobhadsa
Seal beag gairid
I measc mo dhaoine
Ar oileán mara,
Ag siúl cois cladaigh
Maidin is tráthnóna
Ó Luan go Satharn
    Thiar ag baile.

Faoiseamh a gheobhadsa
Seal beag gairid
I measc mo dhaoine,
Ó chrá croí,
Ó bhuairt aigne,
Ó uaigneas duairc,
Ó chaint ghontach,
    Thiar ag baile.

Peace

Peace I'll find
For a short while
Among my people
On a sea island,
Walking the shore
Morning and evening
Monday to Saturday
  Home in the West.

Peace I'll find
For a short while
Among my people,
From a heavy heart,
From a troubled mind,
From dour loneliness,
From hurtful talk,
  Home in the West.

Do Thonn Bheag

A thonn bheag fhann,
A ghluaiseas go mall
Ag triall duit ar thráigh.

Ní heol duit do thús
Is ní dod' dheoin
A ghluaisis chun cinn
Ar dhroim mhór na bóchna.

Ní fada do ré,
Óir ar ghainimh na trá,
Is cúr bán do dheireadh.

Ach ná bí in éad
Leis an tonn mhór thréan;
Cé nárbh ard do ghlór
Rinnis do dhícheall,
Is cúr ar thráigh
A deireadh siúd freisin.

To a Tiny Wave

Weak and tiny wave
Slowly rolling in
On your way to the shore,

You don't know your genesis
And it's not of your own free will
That you roll along
On the vast back of the ocean.

And your time is not long,
For you end up as foam
On a sandy beach.

But do not envy
Any high and mighty waves:
Your voice may not have rung out
To the skies
But you did the best you could,
And foam on a beach
Is how they end up, too.

from

DÁNTA ANIAR

[Poems from the West]

(1943)

Dínit an Bhróin

Nochtaíodh domsa tráth
Dínit mhór an bhróin,
Ar fheiceáil dom beirt bhan
Ag siúl amach ó shlua
I bhfeisteas caointe dubh
Gan focal astu beirt:
D'imigh an dínit leo
Ón slua callánach mór.

Bhí freastalán istigh
Ó línéar ar an ród,
Fuadar faoi gach n-aon,
Gleo ann is caint ard;
Ach an bheirt a bhí ina dtost,
A shiúil amach leo féin
I bhfeisteas caointe dubh,
D'imigh an dínit leo.

The Dignity of Grief

Laid bare to me once
Was grief's great dignity,
The time I saw two women
Walking out of a crowd
In their black funeral clothes,
Neither speaking a word:
Dignity went with them
From the loud, vulgar throng.

A tender had come in
From a liner off the shore,
There was jostling and shouting,
People rushing around;
But the two who were silent
And walked off together
In their black funeral clothes,
Dignity went with them.

Tnúth

Dhruideas na dallóga aréir
Ar fhuinneog mo sheomra,
Is mhúchas gach solas
Ach fannsolas gríosaí,
Gur tháinig do chumraíocht
Chugam do m'aoibhniú:
D'aghaidh chaoin gheanmnaí
A léirigh d'anam geal,
Is na lámha is áille
Dá bhfuil ar aon mhnaoi.
Déanfad amhlaidh go minic feasta,
Óir is tusa domsa
An tseoid dhofhála:
    Is níos gaire ná sin
    Ní bheir go brách dom.

Longing

Last night I shut the blinds
On my bedroom window
And put out every light
But the fire's dying embers,
Until your image came
Filling me with joy:
Your face pure and innocent,
The window to your soul,
And the loveliest hands
On any woman. From now,
I'll do the same thing often
For you're the unobtainable
Jewel just out of reach:
  And you will never be
  Nearer to me again.

Cuimhní Cinn

Maireann a gcuimhne fós i m'aigne:
Báininí bána is léinte geala,
Léinte gorma is veistí glasa,
Treabhsair is dráir de bhréidín baile
Bhíodh ar fheara cásacha aosta
Ag triall ar an Aifreann maidin Domhnaigh
De shiúl cos ar aistear fhada,
A mhúsclaíodh i m'óige smaointe ionamsa
Ar ghlaine, ar úire, is fós ar bheannaíocht.

Maireann a gcuimhne fós i m'aigne:
Cótaí cóirithe fada dearga,
Cótaí gorma le plúirín daite,
Seálta troma aníos as Gaillimh,
Bhíodh ar mhná pioctha néata
Ag triall ar an Aifreann mar an gcéanna;
Is cé go bhfuilid ag imeacht as faisean,
Maireann a gcuimhne fós i m'aigne
Is mairfidh cinnte go dté mé i dtalamh.

Memories

Their memory lives on in my mind:
White *báiníns* and clean pressed shirts,
Sky-blue shirts and stone-grey waistcoats,
Trousers and drawers of homemade tweed
Worn by venerable old men
On their long walk to Sunday Mass,
Stirring thoughts in my young self
Of cleanness, purity, and piety.

Their memory lives on in my mind:
Long red petticoats neatly gathered,
Sea-blue skirts dyed with indigo,
Heavy shawls brought over from Galway
On women arrayed in their Sunday best,
Making their way to Mass, too;
And though they're going out of fashion,
Their memory lives on in my mind
And will live for sure until I'm buried.

from

ROGHA DÁNTA

[Selected Poems]

(1949)

Maidin Domhnaigh

Mo sheanmháthair ar a glúine
Sa reilig ag urnaí
Maidin Domhnaigh gréine,
Is monabhar a guidhe
Á mheascadh go cumhra
Le crónán na ndúl beag aerga.

Féileacán ildaite
Is a ghlóir-réim á leathadh
Ar eite na leoithe séimhe,
Is dhearmad mé paidir
Mo sheanmháthar a fhreagairt
Is leanas le haiteas an t-iontas.

Sunday Morning

My grandmother kneeling
To pray in the graveyard
One sunny Sunday morning,
And the murmur of her prayer
Blending in sweetly
With the humming of airborne mites.

On the wing of a gentle breeze,
A rainbow-colored butterfly
Widened its glorious realm,
And I forgot the response
To my grandmother's prayer,
Carried away by the wonder.

Óige an Fhile

Bhínn ag déanamh fear de chlocha
Is á gcur go léir ag ól,
Ní bhíodh fear ar an mbaile
Nach mbíodh samhail agam dó.

Bhíodh na comharsain ag magadh fúm,
Is mo mháthair de shíor ag bagairt orm,
Ach níor thuigeadar ar aon chor mé,
An buachaill aisteach ciúin.

Ghreamaigh díom an galar úd
Is ní saor mé uaidh go fóill,
Is é a sheol ar bhóthar na n-aisling mé
Is a dhealaigh mé ón sló.

The Poet as a Young Man

I'd make men out of rocks
And set them up drinking.
There wasn't a local man
Whose image I hadn't down.

The neighbors used to mock
And my mother warned me
But they didn't understand
The strange, quiet boy.

The affliction stuck with me
And I'm not free of it yet.
It set me chasing visions
And split me from the crowd.

Rún na mBan

Tráthnóna Domhnaigh ab ionduala
Ansiúd iad cois tine,
Ná mná agus na seálta
Casta ar a gcloigne,
Bhíodh tae ann i gcónaí
Ar ócáid den chineál,
Is braon ag dul thart de
Ó dhuine go duine.

Thosaíodh an chaint
An broideadh is an sioscadh,
Uille ar ghlúin ag cur leis na focla;
D'ordaítí mise amach ar na bóithre,
Gan a bheith istigh ag slogadh gach focail,
Go mba folláine amuigh mé
Ar nós mo leithéid eile.

D'imínn sa deireadh,
M'aghaidh lasta is mé gonta
Ach is mairg nach bhfanainn:
Nuair a smaoiním anois air
Cá bhfios cén rúndiamhair
Nach eol d'aon fhear beirthe
A phiocfainn ó mhná
Scartha thart ar thine,
Iad ag ól tae
Is seálta ar a gcloigne?

The Women's Secret

On Sunday evenings usually,
They'd be there by the fire,
The women with their shawls
Wrapped over their heads;
And on such occasions,
There'd always be a drop
Of tea passed around.

Then the talking would start,
The nudging and whispering,
Elbow on knee for emphasis;
I'd get my marching orders,
"You'd be better off out
With kids your own age
Than stuck around here
Taking in every word!"

I'd go, eventually,
All hurt and red in the face.
Shame is, I didn't stay.
For, now that I think of it,
Who can tell what mystery
(Known to no man born)
I would have gathered from them,
The women spread around the fire,
Drinking tea together
With shawls over their heads?

Stoite

Ár n-aithreacha bhíodh,
Is a n-aithreacha siúd,
In achrann leis an saol
Ag coraíocht leis an gcarraig loim.

Aiteas orthu bhíodh
Tráth ab eol dóibh
Féile chaoin na húire,
Is díocas orthu bhíodh
Ag baint ceart
De neart na ndúl.

Thóg an fear seo teach
Is an fear úd
Claí nó fál
A mhair ina dhiaidh
Is a choinnigh a chuimhne buan.

Sinne a gclann,
Is clann a gclainne,
Dúinn is éigean
Cónaí a dhéanamh
In árais ó dhaoine
A leagfadh cíos
Ar an mbraon anuas.

Beidh cuimhne orainn go fóill:
Beidh carnán trodán
Faoi ualach deannaigh
Inár ndiaidh in Oifig Stáit.

Uprooted

Our fathers
And their fathers before them
Grappled with life,
Wrestling the bare rock.

Bliss was theirs
When they encountered
Nature's beneficence,
And zeal was theirs
As they withstood
The power of the elements.

One man built a house,
And another man
A dyke or dry-stone wall
That outlived him
And preserved his memory.

We, their children,
And their children's children,
Must hole up
In private rentals
Where the landlord
Would charge money
For the damp on the walls.

We'll be remembered yet:
A pile of papers
Buried in dust,
Left behind
In a Govt. office.

An tEarrach Thiar

Fear ag glanadh cré
De ghimseán spáide
Sa gciúnas séimh
I mbrothall lae:
    Binn an fhuaim
    San Earrach thiar.

Fear ag caitheamh
Cliabh dá dhroim,
Is an fheamainn dhearg
Ag lonrú
I dtaitneamh gréine
Ar dhuirling bhán:
    Niamhrach an radharc
    San Earrach thiar.

Mná i locháin
In íochtar díthrá,
A gcótaí craptha,
Scáilí thíos fúthu:
    Támhradharc sítheach
    San Earrach thiar.

Tollbhuillí fanna
Ag maidí rámha,
Currach lán éisc
Ag teacht chun cladaigh
Ar órmhuir mhall
    I ndeireadh lae;
    San Earrach thiar.

Springtime in the West

A man scraping clay
From the tread of a spade
In the peace and calm
Of a warm day:
  Sweet the sound
  Of Springtime in the West.

A man slinging
A creel from his back
And the red mayweed
Glistening
In a ray of sunlight
On a white stony beach:
  A shimmering vision
  Of Springtime in the West.

Women standing,
Their coats tucked up,
The ebb-tide pools
Like mirrors beneath them:
  A dreamy sight,
  Springtime in the West.

The hollow beat
Of oar strokes,
A currach full of fish
Coming in to shore
On a slow, gold sea
  When day is done:
  Springtime in the West.

(trans. Peter Sirr and Frank Sewell)

Árainn 1947

Feadaíl san oíche
Mar dhíon ar uaigneas,
Mar fhál idir croí is aigne
Ar bhuairt seal,
Ag giorrú an bhealaigh
Abhaile ó chuartaíocht,
An tráth seo thiar
    Níor chualas.

Amhrán aerach,
Scaradh oíche is lae,
Ó ghroífhear súgach,
Gaisce ard is goití dúshláin
Is gach uaill mhaíte
Ag scoilteadh clár an chiúnais,
Tráth a mbíodh gníomha gaile a shinsear
Á n-aithris do dhúile an uaignis,
An tráth seo thiar
    Níor chualas.

Liú áthais ná aitis
Ó chroí na hóige
Ag caitheamh "cloch neart"
Mar ba dhual tráthnóna Domhnaigh,
Nó ag cur liathróid san aer
Le fuinneamh an bhuailte,
An tráth seo thiar
    Níor chualas.

Ní don óige feasta
An sceirdoileán cúng úd.

Aran 1947

Whistling in the night
To ward off apprehension,
To block out sorrow a while
From the heart and mind,
To shorten the road
Back home from visiting,
This time in the West,
  I never heard.

A boisterous ballad,
At break of day,
From a hearty drunk,
Bigging it up,
His every yell
Splitting the silence
With tales of his forebears,
Their doughty deeds
Relayed to the four winds,
This time in the West,
  I never heard.

A shout of joy or excitement
From the heart of the young
Throwing a shot-put stone,
A Sunday-evening tradition,
Or striking a ball into the air
With force behind the blow,
This time in the West,
  I never heard.

Not for the young anymore,
That narrow, wind-scoured island.

from

Ó MÓRNA

(1957)

Ó Mórna

A ródaí fáin as tír isteach
A dhearcann tuama thuas ar aill,
A dhearcann armas is mana,
A dhearcann scríbhinn is leac,
Ná fág an reilig cois cuain
Gan tuairisc an fhir a bheith leat.

Cathal Mór Mac Rónáin an fear,
Mhic Choinn Mhic Chonáin Uí Mhórna,
Ná bí i dtaobh le comhrá cáich,
Ná le fíor na croise á ghearradh
Ar bhaithis chaillí mar theist an fhir
A chuaigh in uaigh sa gcill sin.

Ná daor an marbh d'éis cogar ban,
D'éis lide a thit idir uille
Is glúin ar theallach na sean,
Gan a phór is a chró do mheas,
A chéim, a réim, an t-am do mhair,
Is guais a shóirt ar an uaigneas.

Meas fós dúchas an mhairbh féin
D'eascair ó Mhórna mór na n-éacht,
Meabhraigh a gcuala, a bhfaca sé,
Ar a chuairt nuair a d'éist go géar,
Meabhraigh fós nár ceileadh duais air,
Ach gur ghabh chuige gach ní de cheart.

Chonaic níochán is ramhrú dá éis,
Chonaic mná ag úradh bréidín,
Gach cos nocht ó ghlúin go sáil
Ina slis ag tuargain an éadaigh,
Bean ar aghaidh mná eile thall
Ina suí suas san umar bréige.

Ó Mórna[1]

Dear traveler blown in from the mainland
Who spies a gravestone on a cliff,
Who spies a coat of arms and motto,
Who spies a legend carved in stone,
Don't leave the graveyard near the bay
Without hearing the man's story.

His name was Cathal the Great Mac Rónáin,
Son of Conn Mac Conáin Ó Mórna,
But do not trust the general consensus
Or old women blessing themselves
As faithful testament to the man
Buried in that graveyard soil.

Don't damn the dead on women's whispers
Or hints let fall twixt elbow and knee
By old folks gathered round a fire,
Without considering his blood and breed,
His rank and station, the time he lived,
The dangers of isolation to his kind.

Consider, too, the dead man's background:
A direct descendant of Mórna the Mighty,
He took in all he saw and heard,
Listening closely on his rounds;
Nor was he denied any prize
But claimed it all as his birthright.

He stood and watched the women washing,
Fulling and tucking the homespun cloth,
From knee to heel each leg uncovered,
Pounding the tweed like a wash-staff—
The women sitting facing each other
On either side of a handmade trough.

Chonaic is bhreathnaigh gach slis ghléigeal,
Chonaic na hógmhná dá fhéachaint,
Dá mheas, dá mheá, dá chrá in éineacht.
D'fhreagair fuil an fhireannaigh thréitheach,
Shiúil sí a chorp, las a éadan,
Bhrostaigh é go mear chun éilimh.

"Teann isteach leo mar a dhéanfadh fear,
Geallaimse dhuit go dteannfar leat,
Feasach iad cheana ar aon nós,
Nach cadar falamh gan géim tú,
Ach fear ded' chéim, ded' réim cheart."
Pádhraicín báille a chan an méid sin,
Briolla gan rath! Mairg a ghéill dó.

Iar ndul in éag don triath ceart
Rónán Mac Choinn Mhic Chonáin,
Ghabh Cathal chuige a chleacht,
A thriúcha is a chumhachta
A mhaoir, a bháillí go dleathach,
A theideal do ghabh, is a ghlac.

An t-eolas a fuair sna botháin,
Nuair a thaithigh iad roimh theacht i seilbh,
Mheabhraigh gach blúire riamh de,
Choigil is choinnigh é go beacht,
Chuaigh chun tairbhe dó ina dhiaidh sin
Nuair a leag ar na daoine a reacht.

Mheabhraigh sé an té bhí uallach,
Nach ngéillfeadh go réidh dá bheart,
Mheabhraigh sé an té bhí cachtúil,
An té shléachtfadh dó go ceart,
Mheabhraigh fós gach duais iníonda
Dár shantaigh a mhian ainsrianta.

He lingered over each pure-white wash-staff
Caught young women looking at him,
Sizing, weighing, riling him up.
His manly blood answered readily,
Traveled his body, reddened his brow
And quickly sped him into action.

"Squeeze up to them, if you're a man,
I promise you they'll squeeze right back.
And anyway, they know full well
You're not some mincing nancy-boy
But a man of power and means."
Thus spoke Paudeen, bailiff and waster.
Woe to any who paid him heed.

Before the rightful lord, Rónán
Son of Conn Mac Chonáin, was dead,
Cathal assumed his father's role,
Seized his districts and his powers,
Took legal possession of his servants,
Bailiffs, title and all he owned.

The insight Cathal gained in the cabins
He used to visit before he ruled,
He now turned over in his mind,
Keeping every bit intact,
Then using it to his advantage,
Laying the law down on his people.

He called to mind the one with pride,
Who wouldn't put up with all his tricks,
He called to mind the spineless lackey
Who'd bow and scrape in due obedience,
He called to mind each maidenhead
His wild desire had ever craved.

Mhair ár dtriath ag cian dá thuargain,
Ba fánach é ar oileán uaigneach,
Cara cáis thar achar mara
B'annamh a thagadh dá fhuascailt,
Is théadh ag fiach ar na craga
Ag tnúth le foras is fuaradh.

Comhairlíodh dó an pósadh a dhéanamh
Le bean a bhéarfadh dó mar oidhre
Fireannach dlisteanach céimeach
Ar phór Uí Mhórna na haibhse,
Seach bheith dá lua le Nuala an Leanna,
Peig na hAirde is Cáit an Ghleanna.

An bhean nuair a fuair Ó Mórna í
Níor rug aon mhac, aon oidhre ceart;
Níor luigh Ó Mórna léi ach seal,
Ba fuar leis í mar nuachair;
Ina cuilt shuain ní bhfuair a cheart,
É pósta is céasta go beacht.

Imíonn Ó Mórna arís le fuadar,
Thar chríocha dleathacha ag ruathradh,
Ag cartadh báin, ag cartadh loirg,
Ag treabhadh faoi dheabhadh le fórsa,
Ag réabadh comhlan na hóghachta,
Ag dul thar teorainn an phósta.

Ag réabadh móide is focail
Ag réabadh aithne is mionna,
A shúil thar a chuid gan chuibheas,
Ag éisteacht cogar na tola
A mhéadaigh fothram na fola,
Ina rabharta borb gan foras.

Stranded on a remote island,
Our master suffered bouts of gloom;
Rarely would a kindred spirit
Cross the sea to comfort him
And so he hunted on the crags
To calm and cool himself down.

Soon he was advised to marry
A woman who'd provide as heir
A legitimate son of noble rank,
Of the seed of Mighty Ó Mórna;
And not be known for alehouse Nuala,
Peg-of-the-heights and Kat-of-the-glen.

The woman, when Ó Mórna got her,
Bore him no son, no proper heir.
He only lay with her a while,
Finding her frigid as a spouse,
Finding himself wed and wretched,
Unsatisfied upon her sheets.

Ó Mórna hurried away again,
Rampaging beyond all legal bounds,
Rooting in tilled and virgin soil,
Ploughing away with force and haste,
Despoiling and deflowering maidens,
Breaking every marriage bond.

By violating oaths and vows,
Promises and holy commandments,
Coveting what wasn't his,
And heeding the will's own whisperings,
He raised the volume of his blood
Into an uncontrollable tide.

Ceasach mar mheasadh den chré lábúrtha
Leanadh Ó Mórna cleacht a dhúchais,
Thógadh paor thar chríocha aithnid,
Go críocha méithe, go críocha fairsing,
Dhéanadh lá saoire don subhachas
Dhéanadh lá saoire don rúpacht.

Maoir is báillí dó ag fónamh
Ag riaradh a thriúcha thar a cheann,
Ag comhalladh a gcumhachta níor shéimh,
Ag agairt danaide ar a lán,
An t-úll go léir acu dóibh féin
Is an cadhal ag gach truán.

Sloinnte na maor a bheirim díbh,
Wiggins, Robinson, Thomson, agus Ede,
Ceathrar cluanach nár choigil an mhísc,
A thóg an cíos, a dhíbhir daoine,
A chuir an dílleacht as cró ar fán,
A d'fhág na táinte gan talamh gan trá.

Níor thúisce Ó Mórna ar ais
Ar an talamh dúchais tamall
Ná chleacht go mear gach beart
Dár tharraing míchlú cheana air:
Treabhadh arís an chré lábúrtha,
Bheireadh dúshlán cléir is tuata.

Tháinig lá ar mhuin a chapaill
Ar meisce faoi ualach óil,
Stad in aice trá Chill Cholmáin
Gur scaip ladhar den ór le spórt,
Truáin ag sciobadh gach sabhrain
Dár scaoil an triath ina dtreo.

Fed up, they thought, with laboring flesh,
Ó Mórna followed ancestral custom,
Leaving behind familiar ground
For fresh new places, far-flung lands,
Devoting days to sheer indulgence,
Devoting days to wild debauch.

The stewards and bailiffs serving him,
Overseeing on his behalf,
Wielded power without compassion,
Causing many a grievous loss;
With all the apple for themselves
And only the peelings for the poor.

Those stewards' names I'll give you now:
Wiggins, Robinson, Thomson, Ede—
Four cheats who never held back malice,
With rent increases, house evictions,
Throwing the orphan out on his ear
And hundreds off their land and shore.

Shortly after Ó Mórna returned
Once more to his homeland for a while,
He fell back to the same old tricks
That made him infamous before,
Ploughing again the laboring flesh,
Defying the clergy and the laity.

High upon his horse one day,
As drunk and bloated as a lord,
He stopped nearby Cill Colmán strand,
To scatter a handful of coins for fun.
Wretches scrambled for every sovereign
The master flung in their direction.

Do gháir Ó Mórna is do bhéic,
Mairbh a fhualais sa reilig thuas
Ní foláir nó chuala an bhéic;
Dhearbhaigh fós le draothadh aithise
Go gcuirfeadh sabhran gan mhairg
In aghaidh gach míol ina n-ascaill.

Labhair an sagart air Dé Domhnaigh,
Bhagair is d'agair na cumhachta,
D'agair réabadh na hóghachta air,
Scannal a thréada d'agair le fórsa,
Ach ghluais Ó Mórna ina chóiste
De shodar sotail thar cill.

D'agair gach aon a dhíth is a fhoghail air,
D'agair an ógbhean díth a hóghachta air,
D'agair an mháthair fán a háil air,
D'agair an t-athair talamh is trá air,
D'agair an t-ógfhear éigean a ghrá air,
D'agair an fear éigean a mhná air.

Bhí gach lá ag tabhairt a lae leis,
Gach bliain ag tabhairt a leithéid féin léi,
Ó Mórna ag tarraingt chun boilg chun léithe
Chun cantail is seirbhe trína mheisce,
Ag roinnt an tsotail ar na maoir
Ach an chruimh ina chom níor chloígh.

Nuair a rug na blianta ar Ó Mórna,
Tháinig na pianta ar áit na mianta:
Luigh sé seal i dteach Chill Cholmáin,
Teach a shean i lár na coille,
Teach nár scairt na grásta air,
Teach go mb'annamh gáire ann.

Declaring with a smile of derision
He'd happily pay a sovereign coin
For every louse under their armpits,
Ó Mórna laughed and shouted out;
His family dead must have heard him,
Buried in the graveyard above.

The curate preached against him on Sunday,
Summoned the powers of heaven against him,
Blasted him for raping virgins
And scandalizing the congregation,
But Ó Mórna trotted proudly by
On his horse and trap past the church.

Each one condemned him for their ruin:
Young women for lost maidenhead,
Mothers for their children's exile,
Fathers for stolen land and shore,
Young men for the rape of sweethearts,
Husbands for the rape of wives.

Each day was followed by another,
Month by month, year by year,
Ó Mórna growing fat and grey,
More surly and sour with every drink,
Barking orders at his stewards,
But never mastering the worm within.

And when the years caught up with him,
He "ached in the places he used to play,"
And lay a while in Cill Colmán House,
His ancestral pile deep in the woods,
A house that grace had never called on,
A house where laughter was rarely heard.

Trí fichid do bhí is bliain le cois,
Nuair a cuireadh síos é i gCill na Manach
D'éis ola aithrí, paidir is Aifreann;
I measc a shean i gCill na Manach
I dteannta líon a fhualais,
Ar an tuama armas is mana.

An chruimh a chreim istigh san uaigh tú,
A Uí Mhórna mhóir, a thriath Chill Cholmáin,
Níorbh í cruimh do chumais ná cruimh d'uabhair
Ach cruimh gur cuma léi íseal ná uasal.
Go mba sámh do shuan sa tuama anocht
A Chathail Mhic Rónáin Mhic Choinn.

Three score years and one he was
When laid in clay at the "monk's church,"
With Last Rites, a prayer and Mass,
Among his people at Cill na Manach,
Along with all his ancestors,
Their coat of arms and motto on the tomb.

The worm that gnawed you in the grave,
Great Ó Mórna, Lord Cill Colmán,
Was not the worm of your power or pride
But a worm that heeds not caste or class.
Sleep soundly in your tomb tonight,
Cathal, son of Rónán Mac Choinn.

Gleic Mo Dhaoine

Cur in aghaidh na hanacra
Ab éigean do mo dhaoine a dhéanamh,
An chloch a chloí, is an chré
Chrosanta a thabhairt chun míne,
Is rinne mo dhaoine cruachan,
Is rinne clann chun cúnaimh.

Dúshlán na ndúl a spreag a ndúshlán,
Borradh na fola is súil le clann ar ghualainn
A thug ar fhear áit dorais a bhriseadh
Ar bhalla theach a dhúchais,
Ag cur pota ar leith ar theallach an dóchais.

Slíodóireacht níor chabhair i gcoinne na toinne,
Ná seifteanna caola i gcoinne na gcloch úd,
Ionas nárbh fhearr duine ná duine eile
Ag cur ithir an doichill faoi chuing an bhisigh;
Gan neart na ngéag ba díol ómóis
Fuinneamh na sláinte is líon an chúnaimh.

My People's Struggle

Fighting against adversity
Was what my people had to do;
Subduing stone and leveling out
The stubborn clay, they toughened up
And raised a family to help.

Nature's defiance made them defiant,
The blood-surge and desire for children
Would prompt a man to smash a doorway
Through a wall in the house he was born in,
Making room for a family of his own.

Slyness was useless against the wave,
And shallow tricks against the stone,
So no one was better than his neighbor
Cultivating the stubborn soil;
As strength declined, their just reward
Was sturdy health and family to help.

Deireadh Ré

Fir na scéal mo léan!
Is an bás á leagadh,
Mná na seál á leanacht
Is mise fós ar marthain
I measc na bplód gan ainm,
Gan "Cé dhár díobh é" ar a mbéal
Ná fios mo shloinne acu.

Ní háil liom feasta dar m'anam
Dáimh a bhrú ar chlocha glasa!
Ní fáilteach romham an charraig,
Mé ar thóir m'óige ar bealach,
Mé i m'Oisín ar na craga,
Is fós ar fud an chladaigh,
Mé ag caoineadh slua na marbh.

End of an Era

The story-tellers, alas!
Death is laying them low,
The shawled women following,
While I am living on
Among the nameless crowd
Who neither know my surname
Nor ask "Who are your people?"

I wish no more, I swear,
To force friendship on grey stones!
For the rock provides no welcome
As I seek my youth on the road,
Like some Oisín on the crags
And all along the shore,
Keening the hosts of the dead.

Bua na Mara

(do Phádraic Ó Concheanainn)

Ní mhairfidh na fir fada
Feasta san oileán rúin,
Ní bheidh neach ar an gcladach
Chun dúshlán na mara a thabhairt;
Cuirfidh an fharraige
An sceirdcharraig úd
Faoina glas-smacht dubhach,
Canfaidh sí a buachaintic—
Sin creill an oileáin rúin.

The Sea's Victory

(*for Pádraig Ó Concheanainn*[2])

The men won't last for long
Anymore on the beloved island,
There'll be no one on the shore
To challenge the sea;
The ocean will take
That wind-scoured rock
Under its grey, gloomy sway,
Singing a victory chant—
The beloved island's death knell.

Cuimhne an Domhnaigh

Chím grian an Domhnaigh ag taitneamh
Anuas ar ghnúis an talaimh
San oileán rúin tráthnóna;
Mórchuid cloch is gannchuid cré
Sin é teist an sceirdoileáin,
Dúthaigh dhearóil mo dhaoine.

Chím mar chaith an chloch gach fear,
Mar lioc ina cló féin é,
Is chím an dream a thréig go héag
Cloch is cré is dúthaigh dhearóil,
Is chímse fós gach máthair faoi chás
Ag ceapadh a háil le dán a cuimhne.

A Sunday Memory

I see the Sunday sun shining
Down upon the face of the land
On the beloved island this afternoon;
Chock-full of rock and scant of clay—
That's the mark of the wind-scoured island,
The hard-pressed homeland of my people.

I see how stone has sculpted each man,
Worn him down to its own shape,
And see the many who left forever
Stone and clay and hard-pressed homeland,
And still I see each bereft mother
Hold onto her children with the bond of memory.

Caoin Tú Féin, a Bhean

Ar an drochuair duit
A tharla i do dháil an fear,
Níor dhea-earra é riamh,
Níor dhea-thuar a theacht.

Rinne cloch de do chroí íogair
Nuair a chuir i do chluais an fríd
A chuir cor i leamhnacht na beatha ort,
A rinne meadhg de do shaol.

D'eascair sé ón dream dorcha
Ar geal leo an oíche,
An oíche is an claonchogar
Bia is beatha dá bhuíon.

Caoin tú féin anois, a bhean!
Cé mall an gol sin agat,
Fadó a chaoin mise thú,
Níl deoir eile agam.

Cry for Yourself, Woman

It was pure bad luck for you
That man happened your way.
He was always a bad article,
A bad sign, anyway.

He turned your tender heart to stone
When he put in your ear the mite
That turned your fresh life-milk sour
And curdled your life to whey.

For he was born of the wicked ones
Who find the night-time bright.
Darkness and the twisted whisper
Are food and drink to his kind.

Cry for yourself now, woman,
Although you left it late;
I cried for you long ago
And have no more tears to shed.

Ómós do John Millington Synge

An toisc a thug tú chun mo dhaoine
Ón gcéin mhéith don charraig gharbh
Ba chéile léi an chré bheo
Is an leid a scéith as léan is danaid.

Níor éistis scéal na gcloch,
Bhí éacht i scéal an teallaigh,
Níor spéis leat leac ná cill,
Ní thig éamh as an gcré mharbh.

Do dhuinigh Deirdre romhat sa ród
Is curach Naoise do chas Ceann Gainimh,
D'imigh Deirdre is Naoise leo
Is chaith Peigín le Seáinín aithis.

An leabhar ba ghnáth i do dhóid
As ar chuiris bréithre ar marthain;
Ghabh Deirdre, Naoise is Peigín cló
Is thug léim ghaisce de na leathanaigh.

Tá cleacht mo dhaoine ag meath,
Ní cabhair feasta an tonn mar fhalla,
Ach go dtaga Coill Chuain go hInis Meáin
Beidh na bréithre a chnuasaís tráth
Ar marthain fós i dteanga eachtrann.

Homage to J. M. Synge

Just what brought you to my people
From foreign luxury to rugged rock
Was something akin to the living clay
And inklings derived from grief and loss.

You never heard the stones' story,
The fireside tale caught your ear;
Nor showed interest in slab or churchyard;
No calling comes from clay that's dead.

But Deirdre appeared on the road before you
And Naoise's currach turned Ceann Gainimh;
Deirdre and Naoise went their way
And Pegeen cursed and swore at Shauneen.

Mostly, you had a book in hand
And, from it, brought the words to life:
Deirdre, Naoise and Pegeen took shape
And leapt, unbounded, from the pages.

My people's ways are in decline,
The wave no longer a protective wall,
But till Cuan Wood comes to Inishmaan,
The words that you compiled once
Will still live on in a foreign tongue.

Teampall an Cheathrair Álainn

A fhothraigh chrín!
A chill an rúin!
Cérbh iad an ceathrar naomh?
An ceathrar álainn úd,
Atá sínte faoi do bhinn.

Ní feas do neach
Cérbh as do thriall
Ná fáth a dteacht ó chéin
Ach gur cheathrar iad
A char an Briathar,
Cuing an Chrábhaidh
Is buarach Dé.

Ní dán dóibh feasta
Tráth ná clog,
Ó leagadar díobh
A gcarcair choil,
Nuair a thiomnaigh siad
Don chré a gcorp,
Is a n-anam do Rí na nGrást.

Tá buannacht ag Dia
Ar an áit ó shin,
Is A shíocháin mar chochall
Thart ar an mball,
Is ní scéithfir a rún,
A fhothraigh chrín.

The Church of the Four Beautiful Ones[3]

Dear ancient ruin,
Church with a secret,
Who were the four saints,
The four beautiful ones
Buried under your gable?

Nobody knows
Their place of origin
Or why they came from afar,
Except that they were four
Who loved the Word,
The harness of faith
And spancel of God.

No more must they rise
For matin or vesper bell
Since they left behind
The prison of the flesh
When they bequeathed
Their bodies to the clay
And their four souls
To the King of Grace.

Since then, God
Has claimed the ground,
His peace like a mantle
Enfolding the place;
And you won't divulge,
Dear ancient ruin,
The four's secret.

Teaghlach Éinne

Fóill, a ghaineamh, fóill!
Fearann tearmainn, seachain!
Cosc do ghnó mall,
Do ghnó foighdeach fág,
Is téadh Cill Mhic Chonaill slán.

Éanna Mac Chonaill Dheirg
Triath Oirialla ba oirearc,
Do thogh an áit mar ionad
Mar scoil léinn don iomad
A chuir a cáil thar críocha.

Fóill, a ghaineamh, fóill!
Stad is lig don bhall,
Fág binn, stua, is doras;
Ní cuibhe ar shaothar Mhic Chonaill
Brat an dearmaid ar deireadh.

Éanna's Household[4]

Hold back, sand, hold back!
Avoid this holy ground.
Halt your slow advance.
Leave off your patient progress
And let Mac Conaill's church stay safe.

Éanna, son of Red Mac Conaill,
Renowned Lord of Oirialla,
Made this place a center
Of learning for the many
Who spread its fame abroad.

Hold back, sand, hold back!
Halt, and let the wall be.
Leave gable, arch and doorway.
Mac Conaill's work does not deserve
To be shrouded in oblivion.

Deireadh Oileáin

Trua bheith fireann ar an uaigneas
Gan ach cian sa teach is duairceas,
Cumas gach fir ag dul chun fuaire
Ó ghlac an cian mar chéile suain.

Má obaid ár mná dá n-ualach,
Má thréigid cré, cloch, gach dualgas,
Dár dhual dá máithreacha a thuargadh,
A ndaoradh ní ceart i mo thuairim.

Má obaid fós do smacht an ghnáis,
Má éalaíd leo ó chogar cáich,
A ndaoradh arís ní cóir dá bharr,
Ní peaca bheith baineann thall.

Tá an saol céadra i ngach áit
Ag meath go mear gach lá,
Fir is an cian ag céadladh de ghnáth
A thuarann go luath a bhás.

Death of an Island

How sad being male in the wilderness,
With nothing but lonesomeness at home,
Each man's vigor freezing up
Since he took sorrow as a bedmate.

And if our women rejected the burden,
Abandoned soil and rock, all duties
That their mothers knuckled down to,
I don't believe it's right to blame them.

If they threw off the yoke of custom,
Escaping all their neighbors' whispers,
Still they shouldn't be condemned;
It's no sin being female there.

Everywhere, the old way of life
Is fading with every passing day;
Men and loneliness cohabiting—
The usual sign the end is nigh.

Leigheas na hEagla

An cuimhin libhse an malrach
A ghoin sibh go deacrach,
Tráth ar chuir sibh thart scéal
Is nath ó dhuine go duine
Is m'athair ag fanacht
Lena chónra chláir uaibh?

Murar cuimhin fós, a fheara,
Ní thógaim oraibh feasta é,
Is gur fadó a dáileadh
Libh féin an chré dhubh,
Is go dtuigim le sealad
Nach bhfuil leigheas ar an eagla
Ach scéal, is nath, is gáire.

The Cure for Fear

Do you remember the young lad
You wounded to the quick
The time you passed your stories
And jokes from person to person,
While my father lay waiting
For you to make his coffin?

If you don't remember,
I won't hold it against you,
For the dark soil was scattered
Over you long ago,
And I have known for a while
That there's no cure for fear
But story, joke, and laughter.

Ár gCuid dá Chéile

Tá cuid agat díom thall,
Tá cuid agam díot abhus,
Ag Áth na Scairbhe fós
Tá cuid den bheirt againn.

Cuid mhór ag Gleann na Smól,
Ag Brí, ag Seanchill,
Ag Gleann Cormaic tá cuid,
Cuid eile ag Gleann Dubh.

Seol anall thar achar mara
Mo dhíchéille féin go beo,
Seol an gad seirce anall
A snaidhmeadh tráth le póg.

Más caolsnáth caite an gad,
Tú féin do spíon é amhlaidh,
Dual ar dhual do spíonais é;
Ar fhigh tú ó shin a shamhail?

Our Share of Each Other

You've some of me over there,
Over here I've some of you,
At Áth na Scairbhe[5] there's still
Some of the pair of us.

There's much at Gleann na Smól,
At Brí and old Seanchill,
At Gleann Cormaic there's some,
And more at dark Gleann Dubh.

Send quickly across the ocean
My madness back to me,
Send me back the love-knot
We once tied with a kiss.

If the knot is threadbare,
You have made it so.
Strand by strand you stripped it;
Did you weave its like again?

Cranna Foirtil

Coinnigh do thalamh a anam liom,
Coigil chugat gach tamhanrud,
Is ná bí mar ghiolla gan chaithir
I ndiaidh na gcarad nár fhóin duit.

Minic a dhearcais ladhrán trá
Ar charraig fhliuch go huaigneach;
Mura bhfuair éadáil ón toinn
Ní bhfuair guth ina héagmais.

Níor thugais ó do ríocht dhorcha
Caipín an tsonais ar do cheann,
Ach cuireadh cranna cosanta
Go teann thar do chliabhán cláir.

Cranna caillte a cuireadh tharat;
Tlú iarainn os do chionn,
Ball éadaigh d'athar taobh leat
Is bior sa tine thíos.

Luigh ar do chranna foirtil
I gcoinne mallmhuir is díthrá,
Coigil aithinne d'aislinge,
Scaradh léi is éag duit.

Strong Oars

Soul, you must stand your ground,
Hold onto all that's deeply rooted,
And don't be like some beardless boy
Needing friends you never suited.

Many times you've seen a redshank
All alone on a sea-soaked rock;
If he got no catch from the waves,
He wasn't criticized or mocked.

From your own dark realm you brought
No lucky caul upon your head;
But wound around your wooden cradle,
Protective bands were overlaid.

Ritual sticks were placed around you,
And iron tongs above your head,
Beside you a piece of your father's clothing,
And in the fire a poker was buried.

Lean upon your own strong oars
Against low ebb and neap tide.
Keep your spark, your vision burning;
Part with it, and you die.

Iascairí an Chladaigh

Fada an seasamh agaibh é,
Cois Teampall Mhuire ansiúd thiar,
Bhur gcúl le tír, is le cill féin,
Bhur súile sínte tar muir siar.

Tá réim an éisc thart le fada,
Sibhse anois iarmhar na mara,
Gach fear mar dhealbh mharmair
Ar shaol bhur sean go seasta.

Éistíg le fead na hadhairce
Ag fuagairt cath ar bhur gcleacht,
Thoir sa gcathair a séidtear í,
Is í creill bhur gcleacht an fhead.

Ná bíodh bhur dtnúth le muir feasta
Ach tugaíg cúl léi go luath,
Tugaíg aghaidh ar chill is ar thír,
Ní fada uaibh anois an uaigh.

The Shore Fishermen

You've held out for a long time now
Near Teampall Mhuire in the West,
Your back turned to the shore and church,
Eyes straining westward across the waves.

The mighty shoals have long gone,
And now you're a relic of the sea,
Each man cast like a marble statue,
A standing image of your ancestry.

Listen to the horn sounding
Its battle cry against your ways.
In the east, the city, it is sounded—
The death knell of your practices.

Don't hanker for the sea anymore
But turn your back upon her soon
And turn to face the church and shore:
You're not far now from the tomb.

Ionracas

Dúirt file mór tráth
Go mba oileán is grá mná
Ábhar is fáth mo dháin;
Is fíor a chan mo bhráthair.

Coinneod féin an t-oileán
Seal eile i mo dhán,
Toisc a ionraice atá
Cloch, carraig is trá.

Integrity

A great poet once said
That an island and a woman's love
Were the subject and the cause
Of my poem. My brother spoke true.[6]

I myself will keep the island
A while longer in my poem
For the sheer integrity
Of stone, rock and strand.

Sic Transit...

Clann Mhic Thaidhg, na flatha
Faoi raibh na hoileáin thiar
Cúig céad bliain go léir,
Síol Bhriain na n-éacht,
An pór teann tréan,
Cá bhfuil a nead cré?

Na flatha a bhris a réim,
A choinnigh a gcion féin
Den talamh garbh gann
Ceithre céad bliain da n-éis,
Gheobhair i reilig thuas ar aill
Leaba a bhfualais is a nead.

Cois cuain atá a bhfeart
Láimh le trá na gceann,
Ar an tuama tá armas greannta
Is mana ar leacht in airde,
Mana a bheireann dúshlán Flaitheartach;
Fortuna favit fortibus—
Ach tá meirg ag creimeadh an ráille.

Tá meirg ag comhrá le seanchóiste
I gclós an tí mhóir le seal anall,
Níl lua ar na flatha ná tuairisc
I dteach a sean ná i gCill Cholmáin,
Ó chuaigh an Flaitheartach deiridh síos
Le líon a fhualais san uaigh láimh le trá.

Sic Transit Gloria Mundi

Clan Mac Taidhg, the lords
Who ruled the western isles
For five hundred years,
Descendants of Brian Boru,
That strong steadfast stock—
Where is their nest of clay?

The lords who overthrew them,
Who kept themselves a portion
Of the rough and scanty soil
For the next four hundred years—
You'll find their resting place
In a graveyard high on a cliff.

Their burial site by the bay
Is near "the beach of heads,"
On the tomb a coat of arms
And, over it, a legend,
The defiant O'Flaherty motto:
Fortuna favit fortibus—
Though rust gnaws at the rail.

Rust and an old carriage
Have been catching up for a while
In the yard of the Big House,
There's no talk of the lords
No tidings in Cill Colmáin,
Or their old ancestral seat,
Since the last O'Flaherty
Was buried with his kinfolk
In the grave by the beach.

Mná na hAiséirí

Umhlaímis go humhal don bhuíon iníonda
A sheas gan feacadh sa spéirling fhíorga
Chun ceart ár gcine a bhaint de dhanair,
Thiomnaigh a ndúthracht, a ndúchas banda,
Thug dílse a gcroí go dil do Bhanba.

Bhí an bhuíon iníonda i dtreo chun seasaimh
Nuair a las an chathair seo seal den ghaisce,
Nuair a ghabh meisce Chásca a príomhshráid seachtain,
Nuair a chuaigh ár leoin chun gleo le Galla,
Nuair a ghairm ar a gcúl na beo is na mairbh.

Nuair a chloígh feadhna an éithigh ár bhfeara,
Nuair a theasc gach bile de chrann na beatha,
Bhí an bhuíon fós ar an bhfód ag faire,
Ag tiaráil chun bua cé dian an treascairt,
Ag coigilt a nirt do lá na faille.

Nuair a tháinig thar toinn anall na hamhais,
Nuair a chuaigh clann na saoirse leo chun catha
Bhí an bhuíon arís gan scíth sa mbearna
Ar fiannas i bhfochair na bhfianna calma
Ina gcranna fortaigh ag clann na gaile.

Ba mhinic iníon go dian i ndainséar
I mbaol a hanama, i mbaol nach n-abraim,
I nguais a duaise ag imeacht ar aistear,
Is scéalta rúin ina comhad go daingean.
Dá dtiteadh le búir don chúis ba mheasa.

The Women of the Rising

Let's bow down humbly to that band of women
Who stood up bravely in the fight for justice
To wrest our sovereignty from the invader;
Dedicating their strength, their female nature,
They gave their love and loyalty to Ireland.

That band of women were ready to make a stand
When this city shone a while with courage,
When Paschal fire lit the main street one week
When our lions went to war with empire
And summoned to their side the living and dead.

When falsehood's troops overthrew our men,
Cut down each scion from the tree of life,
That band still stood their ground, vigilant,
Toiling for victory whatever the danger,
Gathering strength for when their day would come.

When mercenary thugs came over the sea
And freedom fighters went to war with them,
That band of women were tireless in defense,
Serving alongside our brave warriors,
Pillars of support to that clan of heroes.

Many a daughter was faced with grave danger,
Mortal danger and danger I will not say,
Risking her honor going out on a mission
With secret info fastened about her person—
In the boors' hands, a setback to the cause.

Seasaimis dá gclú, dá gcáil go seasta,
Is do cháil na laoch a bhí ina bhfara
Is fuagraímis gach cnáid go críoch an dearmaid,
Gach giolla, gach briolla cunórach dá maireann
Ó táid na leoin faoin bhfód, mo mhairg!

Umhlaímis arís dóibh síos go talamh
Do gach ríbhean dá bhfuil ar marthain,
Is umhlaímis faoi thrí do shlua na marbh
Is guímis Rí na gCumhacht gan dearmad
Luach a saothair a thabhairt thuas ar neamh dóibh.

Let's stand up in support of their name and fame,
And the honor of the men, their *compañeros*;
Commend every jibe to the end of oblivion,
Every slave and revisionist who lives,
Alas, since the lions lie under the sod.

Let's bow once more to them, down to the ground,
Each noble woman who's still living today;
Let's bow three times to the host of the dead
And pray that God Almighty will not forget
To grant on them their just reward in heaven.

Blianta an Chogaidh

Ní sinne na daoine céanna
A dhiúgadh na cáirt,
Is a chuireadh fál cainte
Idir sinn is ár gcrá.

Thuig fear amháin na mná,
Is é a thuig a gcluain thar barr,
An bhantracht go léir a thuig
I gcrot aon mhná nach raibh dílis,
Is sinn ar thaobh an dídin
Den phéin is den pháis.

D'fhaighimis an seic, an giota páir,
An t-ara malairteach fáin,
Ar an saothar aimrid gan aird,
Is théimis chun an ósta ghnáith.

Níor chuireamar is níor bhaineamar
Is níor thógamar fál go hard,
Ach fál filíochta is argóna,
Idir sin is an smaoineamh
Go rabhamar silte gan sinsear,
Go rabhamar stoite gan mhuintir,
Go rabhamar gan ghaisce gan ghrá
Gan aisce don fháistin
Ach scríbhinn i gcomhad.

Is réab gach éinne againn
Cuing is aithne ina aigne;
Aicme a bhí gan fréamha i dtalamh,
Dream narbh fhiú orthu cuing a cheangal,
Drong nár rod leo a n-athardha.

The War Years (1939–45)

We're not the same people
Who would drain the cups
And put up a wall of talk
Between us and our despair.

One of us understood women.
He knew their treachery too well.
All womanhood he recognized
In she who was not faithful,
While we sheltered ourselves
From such passion and pain.

And for our unproductive labor,
That no one paid a mind to,
We'd take the check, the banknote,
That wavering, unstable item,
And head to our usual hostelry.

We didn't sow or reap
Or raise a single wall
But one of poetry and division
Keeping us from thinking
We were spent, without ancestry,
Without roots and family,
Without courage and love,
With nothing to pass on
But some jottings in a folder.

And each of us in his own mind
Severed bonds and connections—
A species lacking in roots,
A band not worth joining,
A brood parted from patrimony.

from

ÁR RÉ DHEARÓIL

[Our Wretched Era]

(1962)

Ár Ré Dhearóil

Tá cime romham
Tá cime i mo dhiaidh,
Is mé féin ina lár
I mo chime mar chách,
Ó d'fhágamar slán
Ag talamh, ag trá
Gur thit orainn
Crann an éigin.

Cár imigh an aoibh
An gáire is an gnaoi,
An t-aiteas úrchruthach naíonda,
Gan súil le glóir,
Le éacht inár dtreo
Ná breith ar a nóin ag éinne.

Níl a ghiodán ag neach
Le rómhar ó cheart,
Níl éan ag ceol
Ar chraobh dó,
Ná sruthán ag crónán
Go caoin dó.

Tá cime romham
Tá cime i mo dhiaidh,
Is mé féin ina lár
I mo chime mar chách,
Is ó d'fhágamar slán
Ag talamh, ag trá
Bíodh ár n-aird
Ar an Life chianda.

Our Wretched Era

A prisoner before me,
A prisoner behind me,
And I in the middle
A prisoner like all
Since we said goodbye
To the land and shore,
And necessity crashed
Down upon us.

Where did they go—
The laughter and the smile,
The warmth, the new-born wonder,
With no hope for glory
Or heroism before us
And no one counting their rosary?

Here no one has
His plot of earth
To dig, no bird
Singing to him
From a branch,
No stream gently
Murmuring.

A prisoner before me,
A prisoner behind me,
And I in the middle
A prisoner like all;
And since we said goodbye
To the land and shore,
Let's turn our attention
To the ancient Liffey.

Bíodh ár n-aire
Ar an abhainn
Ar an óruisce lán
A chuireann slán
Le grian deiridh nóna.

Bímis umhal ina láthair
Is i láthair an tsrutha
Is samhail den bheatha
Ach gur buaine,
Mar is samhail an abhainn
De shráid an tslua
Ach gur uaisle.
An lá is ionann ag mná
Faiche is sráid,
Páirc, trá, is grianán,
Ná bíodh cime gnáis
Gann faoi dhearbhdhíona.

Tá fairsinge díobh ann
Mar luaim thíos i mo dhiaidh iad,
Is deirid lucht cáis
Nach bhfuilid gan bhrí leo—

An macha cúil
Tráthnóna Sathairn,
An cluiche peile,
Ag imirt chártaí
Is ósta na bhfear
Ina múchtar cásamh.

Let's turn our attention
To the river,
The high golden waters
That bid goodbye
To the evening sun.

Let's bow before her
And before the current
That symbolizes life
But is more permanent;
For the river is a symbol
Of the crowded street
Although more noble.
The day when women
No longer distinguish
Between street and lawn,
Field, shore, and suntrap,
Let not the prisoner of convention
Lack means of escape.

The latter are many
—I set them out below—
And those with need of them
Say they're not without use:

The back garden
On a Saturday afternoon,
The football match,
The round of cards,
The gentlemen's bar
Where grievances are drowned.

Crot a athar thalmhaí
Do shúil ghrinn is léir,
Ag teacht ar gach fear
Atá i meán a laethe,
A chneadaíonn a shlí chun suíocháin
I mbus tar éis a dhinnéir.

Ní luaifear ar ball leo,
Teach ná áras sinsir,
Is cré a muintire
Ní dháilfear síos leo,
Ach sna céadta comhad
Beidh lorg pinn leo.

Is a liacht fear acu
A chuaigh ag roinnt na gaoise
Ar fud páir is meamraim,
Ag lua an fhasaigh,
An ailt, an achta.

Is a liacht fear fós
A thug comhad leis abhaile,
Is cúram an chomhaid
In áit chéile chun leapan.

Is mná go leor
A thriall ina n-aice
Ar thóir an tsó
An áilleagáin intrigh.
Galar a n-óghachta
A chuaigh in ainseal orthu
A thochrais go dóite
Abhras cantail.

The cut of his country father
Is clear to the keen observer,
As it settles upon each man,
Now in his middle age,
Panting his way to a seat
On the bus after dinner.

Soon no one will link them
To the home of their forebears,
And the soil of their kin
Won't be scattered over them:
But they'll leave their mark
In hundreds of files.

And many a man
Squandered his talent
On papers and memos,
Citing the precedent,
The article, the act.

And so many others
Took a folder home
And brought it to bed
Instead of a wife.

And many women
Were fellow-travelers
In search of comfort,
Of the must-have bauble;
Their virginity a disease
That turned chronic,
Winding them into
A ball of bitterness.

Mná eile fós
Ba indúilmheara ag feara,
Ba féile faoi chomaoin
Ba ghainne faoi chairéis,
A roinn a gcuid go fairsing
I ngéaga an fhir
Ba luaithe chucu
Ar chuairt amhaille,
Ar scáth an ghrá
Nár ghrá in aon chor
Ach aithris mhagaidh air,
Gan ualach dá éis
Ach ualach masmais.

Na hainmhithe is na héin
Nuair a fhaighid a gcuid dá chéile,
Ní gach ceann is luaithe chucu
A ghlacaid in aon chor.

I gcúiteamh an tsíl
Nach ndeachaigh ina gcré,
I gcúiteamh na gine
Nár fhás faoina mbroinn,
Nár iompair trí ráithe
Faoina gcom,
Séard is lú mar dhuais acu
Seal le teanga iasachta,
Seal leis an ealaín,
Seal ag taisteal
Críocha aineola,
Ag cur cártaí abhaile
As Ostend is Paris,
Gan eachtra dála
Ar feadh a gcuarta
Ná ríog ina dtreo
Ach ríog na fuaire.

Still other women,
Most attractive to men,
Generous with their favor
And lacking in scruple,
Gave themselves willingly
In the arms of the first man
Who came to them
On a sneaky visit,
In the pretense of love
That wasn't love at all
But a pale imitation
Engendering nothing
But a burden of loathing.

Animals and birds,
When they pair up to mate,
It's not the first to come along
That they accept.

To compensate for the seed
That didn't enter their flesh,
To compensate for the child
That didn't grow in their womb,
That wasn't carried full term,
The least that they expect
Is a spell at foreign languages,
A spell at the arts,
A spell running around
In exotic places,
Sending postcards home
From Ostend and Paris,
With no loving encounter
In all their travels,
And no thrill ahead
But the shiver of coldness.

Tá cime romham
Tá cime i mo dhiaidh
Is mé féin ina lár
I mo chime mar chách,
Is a Dhia mhóir
Fóir ar na ceádta againn,
Ó d'fhágamar slán
Ag talamh ag trá,
Tóg de láimh sinn
Idir fheara is mhná
Sa chathair fhallsa
Óir is sinn atá ciontach
I bhásta na beatha,
Is é cnámh ár seisce
An cnámh gealaí,
Atá ar crochadh thuas
I dtrá ár bhfuaire
Mar bhagairt.

A prisoner before me,
A prisoner behind me,
And I in the middle
A prisoner like all;
And God Almighty
Watch over the hundreds of us;
Since we said goodbye
To the land and shore,
Take us by the hand,
Both men and women,
In the hollow city
For we are guilty
Of wasting life,
And the symbol of our sterility
Is the bone-shaped moon
Hanging up above,
In the strand of our coldness,
Like an omen.

Comhairle don Fhile Óg

Níl a fhios agam a mhic
Céard déarfainn leatsa,
Ní peileadóir tusa
Ag teacht faoi chaithréim abhaile,
Ní lúithnire mear thú
Ná dornálaí a rinne gaisce.

Ní bheidh caipíní áiféiseacha
Á gcaitheamh in airde i d'aice
Cé déirc an méid sin
Gurbh fhearr leat ina easnamh.

I dtír inar chuir filí tráth
Tine Chásca ar lasadh,
Ní lastar tinte cnámh
Ar arda do do shamhail.

Glac uaimse is mo bheannacht
Mo chiall cheannaigh,
Ní fearr domsa í agam
Mar ó chaitheas an choinneal
Caithfead an t-orlach ina teannta.

Creimeadh tusa an abhlann
Más leat a bheith ar barra,
Is an méid nach bhfónann duit salaigh
Is abair nuair is caothúil
Gur díth na céille an galar
A bhí ar na móir atá marbh,
Anois nuair nach mairid

Advice to a Young Poet

I don't know, young fella,
Just what to say to you.
You're not some footballer
Coming home in triumph,
A nimble athlete
Or a champion boxer.

There'll be no great show of hats
Thrown high in the air for you—
A pathetic gesture
You're better off without.

In a country where poets
Once set an Easter fire ablaze,
Bonfires don't get lit
For the likes of you.

But take my blessing
And my hard-earned wisdom,
Which hasn't done me much good.
For as I've burned the candle,
I'll burn the last inch, too.

If you're to reach the top,
Sink your teeth into the Eucharist
And desecrate what's left,
If it doesn't suit you.
Say, for expedience,
That lack of sense afflicted
The great who gave their lives.

Ní heagal duit a n-agairt,
Ná leon ar bith
Tríd an gcré dhubh
Aníos chugat ag bagairt.
Caitheadh tusa do dhúthracht
Ar thóir an ríphoist,
Is tabhair tairise don mhodh
Don ghnás don ardú gradaim.

Ach fág a mhic fós
Cion ag an dán agraim,
Mar measaim gur mhór an feall
Nach mbeadh lá éigin feasta
Cuid iontais i do dhiaidh
Ag ollaimh is lucht sanais.

Now that they are dead,
You don't have to fear
Their revenge or any lion
Coming back to bite you
Through the cold, dark clay.

Do everything you can
To get the top-notch job
And pledge your loyalty
To fitting in, networking,
And climbing the greasy pole.

But I ask you, young fella:
Keep some regard for poetry,
For wouldn't it be tragic
If the day came round
When you'd left nothing
For critics and academics
To sit and wonder at?

An Dán á Tharcaisniú

Nuair a thráchtaid ar an dán
An tréad nach áil leo é,
Is nuair a cháinid go hard
Lucht a dhéanta gan fáth
Ach an t-éad a bheith ina gcré,
Is nach dtuigid meon na dtréad,
An té gur mór aige an dán
Lucht a dhéanta is a gcáil,
Ní séanta gur náir leis an scéal,
Ná gur ionann a chás
Is fear a mbeadh a ghrá
Ina hábhar gráisce
I mbéal na bréine féin.

On Speaking Ill of Poetry

When they talk about poetry,
Those who don't care for it,
And when they castigate
Those who actually make it,
For no reason but envy
And failure to comprehend
The independent mind,
Anyone who cares for poetry,
Its makers and their repute,
Cannot but be offended
For they are in the same boat
As the man who discovers
His love being bad-mouthed
By the lowest of the low.

Fear Lasta Lampaí—Gaillimh 1928

Ní raibh sé mór an fear
Níor dheas a bhí ach gránna,
Is cóip an bhaile mhóir
Ag fonóid faoi gan náire,
Ach ghluais gan mhairg fós
Is ar chuaillí chuaigh in airde,
Ba dhraíodóir an fear beag
A raibh an solas ina ghlaic,
É ag tabhairt na gile leis
Ó lampa go lampa sráide.

The Lamplighter—Galway 1928

He wasn't tall, the man,
And not handsome, but ugly,
And the dregs of the town
Mocked him shamelessly
But the wee man ignored them
And climbed upon his ladder,
For he was a miracle worker
Holding the power of light
In the palm of his hand,
Bringing the brightness with him
From streetlamp to streetlamp.

Comhairle Gan Iarraidh

Comhairle a fuaireas tráth
Ó fhear an aon dáin
Gabháil le haistriúchán,
Is go mb'fhearrde mo dhán
An dáil ó thaobh ceirde.

I gcead d'fhear an aon dáin
Ní díobháil ceirde amháin
A choinnigh an duais as mo láimh,
Ach nár abaigh an chré i mo chliabh
Is gur pian linbh a fríth liom.

Unsought Advice

The advice that I received one time
From a one-poem wonder
Was to turn to translation:
"Your poetry would be the better for it,"
He said, "in terms of craft."

With all due respect to the one-poem wonder,
It wasn't a lack of craft alone
That kept the prize from my hand,
But that the clay in my breast didn't ripen,
And my pain was the pain of a child.

Dom Féin

Tar ar do chéill feasta
Tá an leathchéad go tréan
Ar na sála agat,
Níl ribe ar do bhlaosc
Ná meigeall ar do smig
Is bean aosta féin
Ní ghlacfadh dán uait.

To Myself

Wise up quick now.
Your half-century
Is catching up with you.
There's not a hair on your head
Or a tuft on your chin,
And not even an old crone
Would want a rhyme out of you.

Déithe Bréige

Maise a sheanpháiste
A chuir déithe in airde,
Ná tóg ar na déithe
Má léimeadar anuas
Faoi do chosa,
Is má chaith gach dia
A coróin leat aniar
Is an fhonóid ina diaidh
Sna sála ort.

False Gods

So, you old fool
Who set gods on high,
Don't blame the gods
If they leapt down
Under your feet,
And every god flung
His crown back at you,
Mocking and jeering,
Hard on your heels.

Cúram

Garda i mbun a chúraim
Féachann i mo dhiaidh
Is an t-amhras ina shúil;
Leas an phobail gnó an gharda
Mo ghnósa leas an dáin
Is focalbhrat a fháil
Do gharlaigh m'intinne,
Gnó ar leor a dhua
Seach ceannairc is gleo
A shéideadh ina theannta suas,
Ach ní thógaim ar an ngarda
An t-amhras ina shúil,
Mar cá bhfios nach treise
Duine ná daoine fós,
Is é ar a mharana
Go ciúin sa ród.

Duty

A guard doing his rounds
Takes a double look at me
With suspicion in his eyes.
A guard's main concern
Is for the common good;
Mine is for the poem's;
Finding a weave of words
That will fit my brainchild—
A hard enough task
Without the sniping and griping
That blows up all around it;
But I don't blame the guard
For the suspicion in his eyes
Because (who knows?) maybe
Someone on their own
Quietly walking the road,
Deep in thought, is stronger,
Even now, than the many.

An Smiota

An bhlaosc chrón chríon sa scrín
San eaglais cois na Bóinne
Níor bhain an smiota de do bhéal,
Ach b'áil liom a fhiafraí
Céard a thug tú chun na háite
Ó mheasas nárbh údar blaosc chun gáire,
Is cheapas gur rugadh tú in antráth
Is dá mairteá le linn Herod Rí,
Go dtabharfá blaosc an Naoimh isteach
Is aoibh an gháire ort.

The Smirk

The old wizened skull in the shrine
At the church not far from the Boyne
Failed to wipe the smirk off your face,
But what I would like to ask
Is what brought you there at all,
Since a skull is no cause for smirking.
Maybe you were born out of time
And had you lived in the days of Herod,
You would've carried the Saint's head in,
With a smile playing on your lips.

Ceannaithe

Ceist chuirtí tráth
Más fíor na ráite
"Cén áit i nGaillimh
A bhfuil Éire ann?"
Gach prionsa ceannaí
Dár thabhaigh cáil di,
Tá gan oidhre
Ar a áit,
Is b'aithnid dúinne
Toicithe glacacha,
Nach gcloisfear
A dtrácht sa Spáinn.

Merchants

"Whereabouts in Galway
Is Ireland?" was the question
That used to get asked,
If what they say is true.
Every merchant prince
Who added to her fame
Is now without an heir
To step into his shoes.
Meanwhile we have known
Greedy bigmouths who
Will never be heard tell of
Anywhere in Spain.

An Duais

Prealáid ina dhún féin
Manach ina chillín fuarghlas,
Máthairab ina suanlios,
Mise i lios an léinn aréir
Mar a dtagann dán le dua liom;
Íocaimid go léir deachú an uaignis.
Gheobhaidh an triúr an duais fós
Is luach a saothair sa tír uachtraigh,
Ach faighim féin an duais gach lá,
Is luach mo shaothair go dóite:
Gáire an dúiste i mo dhiaidh aniar,
Uaill an choillteáin i mo chluasa,
Is an t-uaigneas suas liom cuachta.

The Reward

The bishop in his residence,
The monk in his cold, grey cell,
The abbess in her dormitory,
And I in my study last night
Where poems come uneasily—
We all pay our tithe of loneliness.
The three of them will get their reward,
Their just deserts in the land above,
But I get my reward each day,
The bitter wages of my trade:
Some fool laughing behind my back,
Some eunuch yelling in my ears,
And loneliness right up to my neck.

Fuaire

Luí ar mo chranna foirtil!
Céard eile a dhéanfainn féin
Ó tá mála an tsnáith ghil
Folamh i do pháirt go héag,
Ach tá a fhios ag mo chroí,
Cé goirt le roinnt an scéal,
Go bhfuil na cranna céanna
Chomh fuar leis an spéir.

Coldness

Lean on my own strong oars!
What else could I do
Since the purse for the bright thread[7]
Is empty, on your side, forever?
But my heart knows all too well,
No matter how much it hurts to say,
That those selfsame oars
Are as cold as the sky.

Dúshlán

Ní tusa, a chait Pangur Bán
Ná mise an té bhí ina dháil,
Ar dhual dó na clanna snáth
A chur gan cháim i ngréasán,
Ach tharla gur tú atá ar an láthair
Beir scéal chuig aon treasachán
Ar gnás leis ár dteanga a shéanadh
Go bhfuil neart inti fós is téagar.

Defiance

Hey there, cat, you're no White Panther,[8]
Nor I the one was with him either,
Whose nature was to weave word-webs
Of finely-bonded clans of thread,
But since it's you that's here (not Pangur),
Tell the news to every whanger,
Who shuns our language or derides her,
That she still has the strength of a tiger.

Éire ina bhfuil Romhainn

An té a nocht a chlaíomh go hard
I do pháirt um Cháisc na lasrach,
Má shíl gur shaor tú ón iomad náire
Nach cuma, óir ní raibh ann ach fear saonta
Is file laochta nár cruinníodh leis stór,
Is nár fhág ina dhiaidh ach glóir;
Cuirfear iallach ort a ghlóir a dhíol,
Faoi mar ab éigean duit roimh a theacht
A bheith i do thráill ag gach bodach anall,
Is má thugtar meas méirdrí arís ort
Bí i do mhéirdrigh mhóir dáiríre,
Is díol a ghlóir is tabhair a sháith
Do gach bodach aniar chun éilimh,
Reic fós a mhian is beir i do threo
Céile nua is a stór chun leapan,
Mar ní tú feasta céile Choinn ná Eoghain,
Céile an Phiarsaigh ná rún na laoch,
Ach más éigean an cumann a chur i gcrích
Agraim thú a shearc na bhFiann,
Gan ceangal leo gan raidhse dollar.

Ireland in the Time Left to Us

If he who bared his sword so high
For you when Easter flamed should find
He'd freed you from such shame in vain,
So what? Wasn't he an innocent man,
A warrior-poet not out for money,
Who left behind him nothing but glory?
Soon, you'll have to sell his fame,
The way you did before he came,
To every Tom, Dick and Henry
Worming his way into our country.
And if they treat you as a whore,
Be the best that cash can afford:
Sell his glory, give what's his
To every dickhead out for business;
Betray his wish and take to bed
Some new mate by the money belt,
For you're no longer Conn's or Eoghan's,[9]
The love of Pearse or Óglaigh na hÉireann,[10]
And since you're bound to seal the deal,
Flower of the Fianna, I beg you, please,
Don't tie a knot with any others
Unless they've got a sackful of dollars.

Mar Chaitheamar an Choinneal

Cheapamar tráth go mbeadh an lá linn
An bua ar fáil, an t-athaoibhneas ag teacht,
Is chaitheamar an choinneal de ráig
Ag fónamh dár gcleacht;
Ní náir linn os comhair cáich
Ár gcloichín ar charn na sean,
Cé gur eagal linn le seal
Go bhfuilimid ag cur gainimh i ngad,
Murar i gCionn tSáile an léin
A cuireadh ár gcleacht ó rath,
Arbh iad na cinnirí críonna
Nó cléirigh an tréis a d'fheall?
Ach mar chuaigh an choinneal go dtí seo,
Téadh an t-orlach ina bhfuil romhainn amach.

Burning the Candle

Thinking that our day would come,
Victory be ours, old joy return,
We burned the candle quickly down,
Doing our bit to serve our culture.
We're not ashamed before the world
Of our pebble on the ancestral carn,
Although we've feared now for a while
We're using a rope to gather sand.
And if it wasn't in sorrowful Kinsale
That our ways were overthrown,
Was it our lackluster leaders or
The treason of the clerks betrayed us?
But in the time left to come,
Let the last inch of the candle
Go the way the rest has gone.

from

CLOCH CHOIRNÉIL

[Cornerstone]

(1966)

Cloch Choirnéil

Is é mo ghéarghuí
Roimh éag dom féin
Go dtiocfaidh fear
De mo chine fáin;
Fear giallteann tréan,
Cloch choirnéil i mballa feidín:
Dá ndeonaíodh Dia a theacht
Ghéillfinn go réidh don imeacht.

Gach feidín má mheasann
Gur cloch choirnéil é féin
Is dán don bhalla titim,
Is ní mhairfidh dá éis
Creat fraigh ná díon
Lindéar ná fardoras.

Cornerstone

My dearest wish before I die
Is for a man of my own exiled stock
To come along, a square-jawed man,
A cornerstone in a wattled wall:
If God grant us such a one,
I'd be ready and willing to pass on.

But if every piece of rubble
Reckons that he's a cornerstone,
The wall is bound to tumble down,
And neither frame nor roof, arch
Nor lintel will be left standing.

Réim na bhFaoileán

Na seabhaic thréana
Ní léir go bhfillfidh,
Is follas nach é
A lá atá ann:
An ladhrán trá
Ná an chorr éisc
An fada eile mhairfidh
Ar chladaí fiara?
Pór na heala
Is an t-éan fionn,
Imeoidh fós ina ndiaidh,
Ach an faoileán amplach
Gona gharbhghlór gránna
Fanfaidh i bhfeighil a choda
In aice an chonúis bhréin:
A mhalairt níor chleacht an t-éan.

A Colony of Gulls

The mighty hawks—
There's no sign
Of them returning.
Clearly, this
Is not their day.
Will the redshank
Or the heron
Last much longer
On sloping shores?
The swan's progeny
And the white sea-eagle
Will next disappear.
But the greedy gull,
With its ugly squawk,
Will stand over its share
Of the rotting remains:
That bird has never
Done different.

Faoileán Drochmhúinte

Is a liacht fear is bean
In Áth Cliath cois Life,
Tuige duit a chladhaire
Féirín a scaoileadh ar fhile?

Coinnigh do phráib agat féin,
A éin an chraois bhradaigh,
Is le do mharthain arís
An file seo ná salaigh.

Leor mar léan liom
Go bhfeicim go seasta,
Gur líonmhaire d'ál
Ná pór ard na heala.

To a Bad-Mannered Gull

With all the men and women there are
In Dublin by the Liffey River,
Why, you rogue, did you have to go
And drop your blessing on a writer?

Keep your crap all to yourself,
Bird with a landlord's appetite,
And never again as long as you live
Target this poet with your load of shite.

It's bad enough for me as it is
To see the way the world has gone:
Your progeny more plentiful
Than the noble brood of the swan.

Cloch is Céir

Seal is leatsa tréith na cloiche
Is tréith na céireach seal eile;
An ionadh leat má d'imigh
Na fir ba ghnáth i do choinne?

Mo chomhairle mura mall uaim é,
An chloch a chur uait is an chéir
Is teacht ar mhalairt béas;
Seal i do bhean níor mhiste.

Stone and Wax

Sometimes you are just like stone,
Other times you are more like wax;
Are you surprised that they have gone—
The men who followed you in packs?

Drop the wax and drop the stone
Is my advice, though it comes late,
And change your whole disposition:
A while as a woman would be great.

Do Easnamh

Drúcht féin den chaonchaint
A d'éalaíodh idir uille is glúin
Dá dtagadh chugat
Ón gcistin tráth a mbídís
Na mná ag cíblis;
Nó focal ón gclós
De ghlór mo dhaoine
Is tú buil do mhuime
Ar leith ón muintir;
Nach mór mar a dhéanfaidís
Do shamhradh a shíneadh?
Is bídís mar chleití
In adhairt do chuimhne,
Nach ngealfaidís an oíche duit?
Ionas nár chás ort feasta
An dúluachair taobh leat.

Something Missing

If just a drop of that dear speech
Let slip between elbow and knee
Should reach you from the kitchen
Where the women used to whisper,
Or a word from the back yard
Carry the voice of my people
To you (fostered out somewhere
And cut off from your own),
Wouldn't it make your summer
Stretch out longer and put a feather
Or two in the pillow of your memory?
Wouldn't it brighten up your night,
So that you wouldn't mind anymore
The deep, dark winter at your side?

Gadscaoileadh

Más beo do bheo dá n-éis
Na gaid go léir a scaoilis,
Is nach corpán ar do chosa thú
Iontach liom mar éacht é.

Gad do dhúchais dual ar dhual
Anuas má ghearrais díot é,
Ait liom i ndiaidh na sceanairte
Más tú atá ann ach iarlais.

Dá gcuirteá an scéal i mo chead
Déarfainn leat a theacht ceart,
Is féachaint go bhfáiscfeá leathghad
In aghaidh gach gaid a scaoilis.

Leathghad a chaitheas i do threo uair
Mar dhúil go bhfáiscfeá aniar é,
Leor eol dom ó shin i leith
I do láimh nár rugais riamh air.

Minic a tháinig de mo dhíomá
Tuairimí agam ort is smaointe,
Nár mhaise dom a dtagairt leat
Dá dtagainn féin ceart i do thaobhsa.

Gaid a scaoileadh ní ionann
Is ualach a ligean síos díot,
Ach i gcuimhne mo leathghaid
Is faoiseamh a ghuím duit.

Breaking Bonds

If you have managed to live on
After all the ties you cut,
And you're not some walking zombie,
Then I don't know how you do it.

If you have cut yourself off
Strand by strand from tradition's loop,
I'd be surprised if, after such paring,
You weren't some changeling but still you.

If you would let me speak plainly,
I'd tell you to catch yourself on
And try to bind just half a bond
For every bond that you have broken.

I once threw half a bond your way,
For you to bind back across;
I know too well that from that time
Your hand never touched it once.

Often, to my disappointment,
I've had opinions, thoughts on you
That I had better keep to myself
If I'm to be fair to you.

Though breaking bonds is not the same
As getting to set your burden down,
In memory of my half-bond,
I hope you find some comfort now.

Comhchríoch

Faoi do mhuintir an diallait,
Is gunna leo chun fiaigh,
Ina lámha an ghlac ó chian,
An sléachtadh rompu, an riar:
An tsrathair ar mo mhuintir féin.

Ar an tseanáit ós áil leat trácht
Cá miste dul i do dháil;
An lá a bhfuil srathair is diallait
Faoi iamh sa mhúsaem
Cá mór nach ionann ár gcás?

Winding Up the Same Way

Under your people the saddle,
And they had guns for hunting,
The reins in their hands for centuries;
They were served and bowed down to—
On my people was the yoke.

Since you like to talk of the old place,
Why don't I go there with you?
The day when yoke and saddle
Are locked up in a museum,
Won't our position be the same?

Berkeley

Ar charraig, a Easpaig Chluana,
A tógadh mise i mo ghasúr
Is bhí na clocha glasa
Is na creaga loma fúm is tharam,
Ach b'fhada uathu a mhair tusa
A Easpaig is a fhealsaimh.

Swift féin an Déan mór
Níorbh ait fós má b'fhíor
Gur fhág tú ar a thairsigh;
Comhla an dorais nár bhrionglóid
I do mheabhair de réir do theagaisc?
Is cad ab áil leis a hoscailt duit
Is gan ann ach a samhail?

An Dochtúir Johnson fós
Thug speach do chloch ina aice
Mar dhóigh go ndearna an buille
Ar an rud ionraic smionagar
De do aisling a chur i gcás
Gur istigh san aigne a bhí
Gach ní beo is marbh.

Ní shéanaim go raibh mo pháirt
Leis na móir úd tamall,
Ach ó thosaigh na clocha glasa
Ag dul i gcruth bríonglóide i m'aigne
Níl a fhios agam a Easpaig chóir
Nach tú féin a chuaigh ar an domhain
Is nach iad na móir a d'fhan le cladach.

Berkeley

On a rock, Bishop of Cloyne,[11]
I was raised as a boy.
Under and all around me lay
Grey stones and bare crags—
A far cry from where *you* lived,
Bishop and philosopher.

Swift himself, the famous Dean,
Was not mad if it is true
He left you standing on his doorstep.
Wasn't the door only a dream
Of the mind, as you had taught?
And why should he open for you
What was only an illusion?

And Dr. Samuel Johnson kicked
A boulder lying next to him,
As though striking the actual thing
Smashed to smithereens your view
That everything alive and dead
Existed only in the mind.

I don't deny my having sided
With those great men for a while
But since the grey stones started
Turning into dreams in my mind,
I'm not so sure, dear Bishop, that you
Were not the one who went on the deep
While the great men stayed on the shore.

Tart an Léinn

"Tóg is léigh," a dúirt an guth
Le hAgaistín sa ghairdín uair:
Cogar ón Spiorad Naomh
I gcluais mhic Mhoinice?
Nó gasúr béal dorais
I mbun a cheachta?

Mac Mhoinice is mé féin
Ní comórtas lá ar bith,
Ná ní cogar ó neamh
Ach tart ceart an léinn
A mheall chun an tobair mé.

Ar shonaide mé an t-oideas,
Nach raibh ar an gcarraig ná a leath,
Nó ar shonaide mé i gceart
Mo dhá cheann i dtalamh dá mbeadh?

Cogar i mo chluais-se cuir
A Mhic Mhuire! is fóir
Go séanad seafóid.

A Thirst for Learning

"Take up and read," the voice said
To Augustine in the garden once—
A whisper from the Holy Ghost
In the ear of Monica's son? Or
Was it just the boy next door
Turning to face his homework?

There's no comparison at all
Between me and Monica's son,
Nor was it a whisper from heaven above
But a genuine thirst for learning
That drew me to the well.

But which would have been better for me—
The education not available
Back then on the island, or
Keeping my nose to the grindstone?

Oh, put a whisper in my ear,
Mary's son! And deliver me
From dullness.

Bí i do Chrann

Coigil do bhrí
A fhir an dáin,
Coigil faoi thrí,
Bí i do chrann.

Coigil gach ní
A fhir an dáin,
Ná bog ná lúb
Roimh anfa an cháis.

Fan socair
Fan teann,
Is fair an uain
Go dtaga do lá.

Corraíodh an ghaoth
A fhir na laoithe
Gach duille ort thuas;
Do stoc bíodh buan.

Uaigneach crann
I lár na coille,
Uaigneach file
Thar gach duine.

Daingean crann
I dtalamh suite,
Cosa i dtaca
Cuir a fhile!

Be a Tree

Store your strength,
Store it times three;
Poetry man,
Be a tree.

Store all things,
Poetry man;
In trouble's storm,
Don't bend or soften.

Stay steady,
Stay strong,
Wait your chance
Till your day come.

Let the wind shake
Your every leaf,
Ballad man,
Your trunk keep.

A tree is lonely
Amid the forest;
A poet lonelier
Than everyone else.

A tree is steadfast,
Fixed in the ground;
So plant your feet,
Poet, deep down.

Coigil do chlí
Coigil d'aird,
Coigil gach slí
I gcomhair an dáin.

Tá do leath baineann,
A fhir an dáin,
Bí fireann, bí slán
Bí i do chrann.

Summon your power,
Summon your senses,
Summon your focus
Into stanzas.

Poetry man,
You're one-half she;
Be safe, be male,
Be a tree.

O'Casey

Níor bheag do ghnó
A dhaingin fhir,
Do thasc níorbh éasca fós,
Den nead seangán
An chloch a thógáil
Den choire bréan an clár.

An peann i do láimh féin
Níor choigeal i láimh óinsí é,
Ag seasamh a chirt don duine
Ar mhór agat a shéan, a shonas.

Éamh an chréatúir is a dhán
Ba ghaire do do chroí lán;
Ná ceobhrat éithigh is camafláis,
Ná seachtarchéim cé ard.

Tart na córa is móríota
Go suífí an ceart i bpáirt,
A chaith do chabhail, a shníomh tú
A d'fhág ár bhfear feochartha ar lár.

A lán dár fhigh tú as cnámhghoin
Níorbh áil le hál an tsámhrith:
Ós deoraí cheana fear na cnise
Ba dheoraí faoi dhó thusa.

An mana ab áil le Heine file
Ós a fheart, a chréchomhad,
Duitse ba chóra thar chách eile
A thug leat stór den daonnacht slán.

O'Casey

Man, yours was no mean feat,
And your goal not easily got:
Lifting the stone from the ants' nest
And the lid from the stinking pot.

The pen that you held in your hand
Was no cudgel in the hand of a fool,
As you stood for the rights of citizens,
Their welfare and the common good.

The cries and conditions of the poor
Meant more to your big heart
Than any smokescreens and distractions,
High renown or taming reward.

A thirst for equality, a zeal
For justice to apply to everyone,
Wore out your body, made you spin,
And burned our firebrand down.

Much that you spun from a deep wound
Did not appeal to the well-off;
But every artist is an exile—
Twice the exile, an artist like yourself.

The legend the poet Heine wanted[12]
Over his grave, his cover of clay,
Befits you more than anyone else,
You who never lost your humanity.

A fhir a d'fheoch le fíoch an chirt
Má d'imigh ón tsine sular chalc do chuid,
Orainne fós abhus a chol
Go bhfuilir i gcéin anocht.

If boiling with rage for justice, you quit
The teat before your share ran dry,[13]
We back here are the ones to blame
That you lie far from home tonight.

Mo Cheirdse

Foighid ar fad mo cheirdse,
Samhail agam iascaire
Ag fanacht le breac.

Breith ar eite éisc
Is fusa ná ar dhán
Is tuile na héigse ag trá.

Samhail agam duine
A chaillfeadh a dheis
Gan breac a bhreith leis.

Cá ndeachaigh duán is baoite?
Cá ndeachaigh dorú is slat?
Is mo bhaisc éisc cár chaill?

Idir dhá chladach
Atáid na héisc uaim,
Idir dhá chleacht
Mo dheis a chaill.

My Craft

It's all patience—my craft.
I'm like a fisherman
Waiting for a trout.[14]

Easier to catch
A fish by the fin
Than a poem
When the tide is ebbing.

I'm like someone
Who has missed his chance,
And come away with nothing.

Where did they go—hook,
Line and sinker, my bait and rod?
Where did I lose my catch?

Between two shores
Are the fish I want,
Between two traditions
My chance slipped past.

Gasúir (cuid a haon)

Criathar chun tobair le gasúir
Nó gad chun gainimh go síor,
Obair nach follas a toradh
Cé ard a torann go fíor.

Spórt is taitneamh na hoibre,
Go deimhin níor mhór linn dóibh,
Is níor dhonaide neach an torann
Ná níor dhochar a n-uaill go deo.

Murach taoille tuile a bheith ag teacht
Go mear orthu aniar aduaidh,
Is gan acu ach píce chun toinne
Cá bhfuil ár bhfeara go beo?

Céard ba chúis le téachtadh?
An bhfuil fuil na bua in éinne?
Nó an leanaí fós ar chéill iad
Go léir ár bhfeara ceannais?

Children (part one)

Going to the well with a sieve
Or using a rope to gather sand—
Their work hardly seems worthwhile
For all the noise and big I am.

Whatever kick they get from the job,
We don't hold it against them;
The noise they make does no harm,
And their vanity is the same.

If a change of tide doesn't come
Unexpectedly and soon,
And they've only a pike against the wave,
Where then will we find our men?

What has caused the congealing?
Is there a champion's blood in anyone?
Or have they all the wit of children,
Our men-in-suits, our politicians?

Tuismitheoirí

Mise athair mo dháin
Tusa féin a mháthair,
Tusa nach bhfeicfidh do ghin,
Gin nach bhfeicfidh a mháthair.

Teagmháil gan gníomh coirp
Síolchur gan treabhadh báin,
An toradh níorbh ualach ort,
Mise a d'iompair an dán.

Parents

I am father of my poem,
You its mother,
You who won't see your child,
A child that won't see its mother.

Intercourse without a sex act,
Sewing without ploughing—
The result[15] for you was no burden,
And the poem mine to bear.

Eala-Bhean

Deireann gach cor is gotha,
Deireann do cholainn uile:
"An bhfuil sibh réidh faoi mo chomhair?"
Is ní túisce cos leat thar dhoras
Ná is leat an duais ó mhná,
Is nuair a théir go héasca thar bráid
Is stáitse agat an tsráid,
Ná ní háibhéil dúinn a rá
Nach siúl do shiúl ach snámh,
Is tráth scaoilir gatha do scéimhe
Ní thagaid ó leanbh go liath slán.

Swan-Woman

Every move and pose of your body
says: "Are you ready for me?"
And the moment you step outside,
You leave all other women behind.
When you pass by with such grace,
You turn the street into a stage.
I tell you no word of a lie:
Your walk's no walk but a glide.
Let loose your beauty like an arrow,
And no one's safe, young or old.

from

CRAINN IS CAIRDE

[Trees[16] and Friends]

(1970)

Boige

An té a thógann máthair
Gan athair ina dháil
Ní rí ar thada é;
Is mogha ar bhoige é.

Ar bhrollach, ar chíoch,
Is bog í a chríoch,
A choisceadh is mall.

Ó bhrollach go cíoch
Is ó chíoch go brollach,
Sin agaibh dán
An té a thógann máthair.

Is tar éis an ghnó
Ar tuirse a leath is níos mó,
Déan gol a mhogha,
Ní miste deoir nó dhó.

An gad imleacáin do chuing,
Go brách ní ghearrfaidh;
An té a thógann máthair
Dar m'anam! gur silte.

Softness

Raised by your mother,
With no father round the place,
You are king of nothing,
A slave to softness.

On bosom, on breast,
You end up soft;
Slow to wean off.

From bosom to breast
And from breast to bosom,
That's the fate of the boy
Raised by his mom.

And after the act—
Of weariness for the most part—
You may weep, soft lad,
A tear or two is appropriate.

Umbilical cord your yoke,
You will never cut it;
Raised by your mother,
You're a softie, I can vouch for it.

Greim Cúil an Dúchais

A ghaoil i bhfad amach,
Col ceathrar mo sheanathar,
Déarfaí faoi do shórt
Go dtugais cúl le dúchas.

Shuigh tú ar an mbinse
Is thugais breith ar do dhaoine
Tráth a dtáinig faoi do dhlínse
D'ainneoin do ghaoil leo,
Is deireadh m'aint go raibh agat
Power dhá ghiúistís.

Ach chuala mé, is tú
Ar leaba do bháis sínte,
Go mba i dteanga Dhónaill an tSrutháin
A bhís ag rámhaillí faoi do mhuintir.

I gcruthúnas go raibh cúig
Fanta fós i láimh an chine,
Is gur nós leis an dúchas
Greim cúil a fháil ar deireadh.

Nature's Backstitch[17]

Dear distant relative,
Cousin to my grandfather,
Your kind, they would say,
Turned your back on your heritage.

When they came under your jurisdiction,
You sat at the bench
And passed judgement on your people
Regardless of your relation;
And my aunt said you'd the power
Of *two* magistrates.

But I heard that, lying on your deathbed,
You returned to the language
Of Dónall from Sruthán[18]
As you raved about your people.

Proof that the hand of our race
Can still play a trick or two,
And that nature has a way
Of getting you back in the end.

An Dá Phortráid

Ní feidir go bhfuilir in éad
Le do leathcheann eile
Ar an mballa os do choinne?

Ba leatsa *Coinnle Geala*
Is *Dánta Aniar* ina theannta,
Snámh smigín ar mhuir an dáin;
Fiche bliain atá eadraibh.

Má tá cúig nó dhó i láimh
An fhir úd thall ar d'aghaidh
Ní gan dua na ceirde a fuair:
Easpa suain is grá gan iarraidh.

The Two Portraits

Surely you cannot envy
Your counterpart there
On the wall opposite?

You wrote *Coinnle Geala*
And *Dánta Aniar*[19] as well—
Floats to hold your chin up
In the sea of poetry;
And there's twenty years
Between the pair of you.

If the man there facing you
Has a few tricks in his hand,
The craft still took its toll:
Insomnia and unwanted love.

Ualach

Ní ualach go hualach uabhair,
Ní uabhar go huabhar file
A fhásann as móiréis na dáimhe:
An fhaid atá tógáil a phinn ina láimh
Tá tógáil a chinn ann,
Is bráithre ina dháil
Ag sníomh le briathra.

Ní umhlaíocht a umhlaíocht
Ach folach priacail;
Is freastal an dá thrá
A chuireann a mheabhair ar fán,
Is a fhágann ina lár
Geit nach den aiteas riamh di.

Ní chuirfí poll ar a onóir
Dá mairfeadh cion ar an mbriathar,
Ach ó chuaigh an briathar ó chion
Is minic ise ina criathar.

Cabhair dá ngoirfeadh Aogán
Níor ghairide dó an ní;
Geallaim nár ghairide fós
Dá ndéanfadh inniu a ghuí.

Burden

There's no burden like the burden of pride,
No pride like the pride of a poet
That stems from the nobility of the calling:
As long as he can hold up his pen,
He can hold his head up, too,
Tangling with words
In the company of his peers.

It's not humility his humility,
But a front to protect himself;
And trying to be two things at once
Drives his mind awry
And leaves deep in his core
A sensation never of joy.

They can't pluck holes in his honor
As long as the word is revered,
But since the word has fallen from favor,
His honor is often like a sieve.

Had Aogán really called for help,[20]
He wouldn't have found it any nearer;
And if he asked again today,
I swear he would get the same answer.

Sólás na Ceirde

Is fiú an sceoin i do lár
Is a tabhairt leat chun leapa:
Donas is fiú gach lá
Más rí ar an bhfocal tú ala.

Géilliúil do chách ní dochar
Ná i do mhogha ag éigean tamall,
Arm faoi ord do dhán
Más géilliúil duit an focal.

Cén dochar an bás i dtráth?
Ná maireadh ach dán amháin
Nó líne a d'aoibhneodh cách
Beirse i do rí ar oileán.

The Solace of Art

It's worth the terror in your core
And that you take to bed at night,
Worth every day of misery,
Be you a king of words at times.

No harm giving way to people,
Or bowing to necessity a while;
Your poem is an army under orders
If words answer to your will.

What matter death when it comes?
If one of your poems still stands,
Or a line that pleases everyone,
You'll be a king on an island.

Achasán

Achasán éigin i ngarbhghlór
A chaith dailtín i mo threo
De dhroim ghluaisrothair:
D'imigh na focail le gaoth,
Is an bhail chéanna a ghuím
Ar a dtiocfaidh eile uaidh.

Mhionnóin go raibh aige féin
Teastas an léinn ó scoil éigin,
Ach geallaimse dósan gan bhréag
Gur chaitheas-sa seal de mo laetha
I dteannta daoine uaisle gan "léann,"
Gan focal dá theanga ina mbéal.

Teastas ní raibh acu ná a dhath
Ach lámh ar an bpeann is a marc,
Ach cheapas a gcaint i mo líon
Mar ba thrua í ligean le gaoth:
Trua eile nár cheapas tuilleadh di.

Insult

From the back of his motorbike,
A young smart-ass cast my way
Some nasty-sounding insult:
Words that the wind whisked away,
And I wish the very same
On all else that comes out of him.

I'd bet you the same fellow
Graduated from some school or other,
But I could tell him no word of a lie
That I passed a portion of my days
Among decent people without "education"
Or a word of his language on their lips.

They had no certificates or such,
But hand on pen, they marked their X,
And I caught their speech in my net
Because it would have been a pity
To let the wind whisk it away.
Pity I didn't catch more of it.

Focalrabharta

(do Chaitlín Maude ó bheith ag éisteacht léi ag léamh a dáin)

Ní bean ná fear tú
I mo mheabhairse, is tú
Ag aithris do dháin,
Más aithris is cirte a rá,
Ach neach de chlann na mara;
A goirme is a glaise
Ag iomaíocht i do shúile
Is tú ag ligean do racht chun fáin
Ina fhocalrabharta.
An scorn leat peann
Ná pár mar áis,
Tráth a dtagann do dhán
Te bruite as do chroí lán?

Word-Tide

(for Caitlín Maude,[21] on hearing her read one of her poems)

You're neither woman nor man,
To my mind, as you recite
Your poem, if recite
Is the right word,
But one of the sea-folk,
Their aqua blue and green
Vying in your eyes
As you let loose
A word-tide of emotion.
Do you scorn devices
Such as pen and page,
When your poem comes
Boiling, bubbling up
From your full heart?

An Gad Stoite

Nuair a théim os cionn staidéir,
Nuair a thagaim ar mo chéill,
Tuigim nach oraibh a chol
Ach ar bhur dtuistí féin,
Nó ar a dtuistí siúd siar,
De dheoin cúinsí crua na staire
Go bhfuil gad imleacáin an chine
In bhur bpáirtse stoite;
Is meabhraím murach fál na toinne
Is iargúlacht mo chine
Go mbeinnse mar atá sibhse
Gan inné agam mar chiste.

The Severed Cord

When I go about my studies,
When I come to good sense,
I understand the fault lies
Not with you but your parents
Or their parents before them,
Due to hard historical facts,
That the nation's umbilical cord
Is severed at your end;
And were it not for the waves' defense
And the remoteness of my people,
I think that I would be like you
With no yesterday to draw on.

Eochair na Foghlama

Tú féin a dúirt a Dhia!
Is cé déarfadh i Do choinne,
An té a d'ísleodh é féin
Go n-ardófaí é go cinnte:
An té a íslíonn é féin abhus
Bail óinmhide is túisce air
Ach ní folamh é dá chionn,
Mar cuireann an chaoi a gcaitear leis
Eochair na foghlama ina ghlaic.

The Key to Learning

You said it, God!
And who would contradict you?
That he who humbles himself
Will surely be exalted...
He who humbles himself here
Is at once treated like a fool
But he is not left empty-handed;
For the way that he is treated
Earns him the key to learning.

Cuing Ghnáis

An fear a chaith splanc ón tine chnámh
Isteach i ngarraí an dorais
Níorbh eol dó athair an ghnímh a rinne;
Ach chomhlíon cuing ghnáis,
A rinne aon chine amháin
De chlann an fhóid anall
Ón Ind go dtí an Sruthán.

The Bond of Custom

The man who carried an ember from the bonfire
And cast it into his own garden
Did not know the origin of his action;
But he carried on a custom
That made one single race
Of every clan of the soil
From India to Aran.

from

CEACHT AN ÉIN

[The Bird's Lesson]

(1979)

Bile a Thit

(ómós do Mháirtín Ó Cadhain)

Fuil na bua a théachtaigh
Is bile ár gcleacht a thit:
Tásc na tubaiste fuaire
A rinne oighear den mheidhir sna fir.

Ba feannta an uair í,
Ba chaillte an mhaidin,
Ar leagadh san uaigh tú,
Is cé nach í cré do mhuintire
A dáileadh síos leat
Ní miste an cumasc duitse
A ghlac chugat Éire uile
Le páirt is tairise di.

Mallmhuir ní luaifear leat
Ná go brách lagtrá:
Ba rabharta a théadh thar maoil
Do bhruth is do chumas;
Ach is olc a théann an rabharta
Ar an mallmhuir dúinne.

Le fíoch ba mhinic a d'fhiuchais,
Truabhail do chleacht
A líon do racht gur scaoil.

Mura ndeachaigh namhaid ná cara féin slán
Ó aghaidh do chraois
Maitear a lán do rí an fhocail;
Maithfear duitse mar sin
I do rí gan freasúra a chuais go cill.

The Fallen Champion[22]

(an homage to Máirtín Ó Cadhain[23]*)*

With our craft's champion fallen,
Our fighting blood ran dry:
News of the disaster froze
Men's natural warmth to ice.

The weather was sharp,
The morning wretched
When they laid you in the grave,
And though it wasn't your family soil
Scattered over you,
Such intermingling befits
You who embraced *all* Ireland
With your loyalty and love.

No neap tide will be associated with you,
And never any ebbing away
For your passion and power
Were an overflowing torrent,
But now your high tide ill befits
Our low.

Often you boiled with rage:
Neglect for your culture
Pushing you till you let fly.

And if neither friend nor enemy escaped
A tongue-lashing from you,
Much is forgiven the king of words;
And so you will be forgiven
Who went to your grave an undisputed king.

Ach ní tú thit ann:
Meirge Mhurchú a thit arís,
Cionn tSáile eile a bhriseadh orainn,
Eachroim an Áir is Scairbhsholais.

But it wasn't you that fell there:
Murchú's banner fell once more,[24]
And we lost another Kinsale,
Another Aughrim and Scarriffholis.[25]

Machnamh an Mharcaigh

Corrach mo shuí anocht
In airde ar mhuin an eich,
Bheith thuas cé go te
Ní deimhin de dar liom
Gur buan dom sa diallait.

Cé tinneasach mé
Ó na mairc a tholg,
Is ó chuimhne na bé
A thabhaigh an siúl dom,
Ní hé is measa ar bith
Ach líonrith ionam istigh
Go mbrisfidh an gad boilg.

Má sciurdaim thar an gcloch
Ná daortar mé dá chionn,
Is gurb é eagla mo thitime
Faoi deara mo shodar.

The Rider's Thought

Unsteady my seat tonight
Mounted on the steed;
To be thus well seated
Gives, I think, no surety
Of my permanence in the saddle.

Sore as I am
From the marks of the mount
And from the memory of her
Who caused me to go,
That's not the worst of it
But the terror within me
That the bellyband will break.

If I dash past the stone[26]
Let me not be condemned,
Since the fear of my falling
Is the reason for my flight.

trans. Máirtín Ó Direáin[27]

Lúb ar Lár

Cloisim taobh liom an comhrá,
Ach ní fheicim an vástbhalla
Ar a leagaidís a n-ucht na mná:
An leathchomhla ní fheicim,
An tuirne ná an cheirtlín snáith.

Ní chloisim an chaint líofa
Ab fhiú a shníomh i ndán:
Idir dhá chleacht is mairg
Gur ligeadh an lúb ar lár.

Dropped Stitch

I can hear them talking beside me
But I cannot see the half-wall
That the women used to lean on;
And I don't see the half-door,
The spinning wheel or ball of thread.

I do not hear the flowing speech
That was worth weaving into a poem:
Between two traditions, alas,
The stitch was dropped.

Cúirt ar Dhán

"Cé mar 'tá an chumadóireacht?"
A dúirt an fear liom go lách;
Culaith ghlas thuas air,
Is scáth fearthainne ina láimh,
"Tar isteach," a dúras féin
"Go bhfeicfidh tú dán."

Ghlac le mo chuireadh go fial
Leag a scáth fearthainne
Go cúramach cois balla,
Shuigh faoi ar chathaoir
Is rinne binse den bhord,
Gur chomhair gach siolla go beacht
Gur thomhais gach líne sa dán.

Ba stór seanfhocal ar a chosa é
Is ba fial faoina stór gach lá,
Ach lá úd na cinniúna
Níor scaoil sé chugam ach ceann:
"Namhaid an cheird gan a foghlaim,"
A chualas as a bhéal go fuar,
Chroch a scáth fearthainne leis
Is bhuail go sásta bóthar.

Cara den namhaid tréan
Ní dhearna mé féin fós
Tar éis tuilleadh is tríocha bliain,
Ó cuireadh cúirt ar mo dhán.

Poem in the Dock

"How's the writing going?"
The man asked pleasantly,
With a grey suit on him
And a brolly in his hand.
"Come on in," I replied,
"And I'll show you a poem."

Kindly accepting my invite,
He set his brolly down,
Carefully, against a wall
And, sitting down on a chair,
He transformed the table
Into a judge's bench,
Scanning every syllable,
Weighing up each line.

A walking store of proverbs,
He always shared them round,
But on that day of judgement,
He issued just the one:
"An unlearnt craft's a foe,"
I heard him say coldly.
Satisfied, he hit the road,
Brolly over his shoulder.

In thirty years and more
Since my poem was tried,
I've still not made a friend
Of my stalwart enemy.

Tusa

Nach iad na gealbháin
A bhíonn dána i Vársá?
Iad go luaineach thart
Ar na boird chruain:
Gach éan ina bhurla teanntáis.

Na gloiní tae ar na boird chéanna,
Agus tú féin ar do bhealach
Go Moscó ar maidin
A thug Chekhov i mo cheann.

Is iad na spideoga
A bhíonn dána in Éirinn
Is a dhéanann teanntás;
Ach cén dochar a thoirtín mná,
Tiocfaidh do chuma chugam
Le ceiliúr na n-éan gach lá.

You

How daring the sparrows are
In Warsaw, bobbing around
On the formica tables,
Each bird a bundle of boldness.

The glasses of tea on the tables
And you making your way
To Moscow in the morning
Reminded me of Chekhov.

In Ireland, it's the robins
Are daring and make bold;
But no matter, *dorogáya*,[28]
Your image will come to me
With birdsong every dawn.

Neamhionraic Gach Beo

Nuair a bhí tine is ól mar dhíon
Ar shíon na hoíche fuaire
Ba bhurla beag beadaí tú
I dteas na tine os do chomhair
Is ó mheidhir an fhíona taobh leat;
Ach d'aird fós ar do ghnó
In ainneoin tine, óil is teasa,
Ach ní rabhais ionraic ar oileán
Ná aon duine den bhuín a bhí i do theannta.

An seantriath ar an mballa
Gona mhéadal nósmhar,
Is a chaofach mná thall
Gona brollach nósmhar,
Atá ceaptha in dhá phortráid

Atá neamhbheo gan malairt
Le trí chéad bliain is breis
Táid beirt ionraic ar oileán,
Mar tá cloch, carraig is trá
I lár na hoíche fuaire.

Sleamhnaíonn nithe neamhbheo
Siar ón mbeo go bhfágann é:
An amhlaidh sin a d'fhág
An t-oileán mo dhán,
Nó ar thugais faoi deara é?

No Integrity Among the Living

When fire and drink were a shelter
Against the cold stormy night,
You were a wee bundle of joy,
With the warm heat of the fire opposite
And a cheering glass of wine beside you;
But your mind was still on other business
In spite of fire, drink and warmth,
So you didn't have the integrity,
The sincerity of an island,[29]
And neither did anyone around you.

The old lord hanging on the wall
With his characteristic paunch,
And his good lady opposite him
With her customary cleavage,
Are captured in two portraits,

Unliving and unchanged
For over three hundred years—
They both have the integrity,
The sincerity of an island,
Like stone and rock and strand
Deep in the cold dark night.

Unliving things slip away
From life until they leave it:
Is that how the island left
My poem? Or did you notice?

Trí Gháire

Stócach faoi ualach cuaile,
Cigire ar an mbóthar is máistir:
Caitheann an cigire leathchoróin
Feadh an bhóthair
Is déanann gáire,
Gáire eile ón máistir.

Cromann an stócach go dtógann
An tabhartas geal ón gclábar
Tráth a ndéanann gáire cásmhar.

Ábhar grinn don chigire,
Ábhar grinn don mháistir,
Ach feiceann an stócach
Cloch phlúir i mála

Is bológ úr i mbácús.

Three Laughs

A young man carrying firewood.
A school inspector and master
On the road before him.
The inspector throws a half crown
The length of the road
And laughs.
The master laughs, too.

The young man bows down to lift
The bright shiny offering from the mud,
Making a forced laugh of his own.

Just a joke to the inspector,
Just a joke to the master,
But the young man sees
A bag of self-raising flour

And a fresh loaf in the oven.

Do Sheán Ó Ríordáin

B'fhada an cath a fearadh
Ar an gcnoc úd thiar
Idir Eachlach Dé is tú féin:
Lámh in uachtar is in íochtar
Gach re seal go dian.

Níorbh aon ghnáthbhé
Ba dhuais ag deireadh an lae,
Ach an bhánbhé
Dár thugais géillsine
Go luath i do ré.

Ó chuiris peann i bhfearas
Chun catha ar scáth na bé
Ní ar uachtar d'imigh,
Ach thochail go dtáinig
Ar do leac féin.

B'ionann do leac
Is leac na bpian
Ar an talamh gach lá riamh,
Mar bhí an máistir go dian
Is tú ag foghlaim an bháis
Gan spás faoina riar
Is an pianfhoclóir i d'aice.

Cad ab áil leat feasta
De phianfhoclóir
Is Foirm na Fírinne
Os do chomhair go seasta,
Go mb'é sin toradh
Ár nguí chun Dé.

For Seán Ó Ríordáin

It was a long hard-fought war
Waged up on that hill
Between you and the Angel
Of God, one side winning,
Then the other.

No run-of-the-mill Muse
Was your final reward,
But the White Goddess
To whom you were devoted
From early in your life.

Since you set your pen
To fighting for her cause,
You didn't keep to the surface
But dug down until you reached
Your own bedrock.

And your bedrock
Was a bedrock of pain
Every day on earth,
For yours was a strict master
As you studied death
Without stint under his stewardship
With the "dictionary-of-pain" by your side.[30]

What need have you now
For any pain-dictionary,
With the Truth itself
Right there before you?
May God answer
Our prayer.

Ós dearfa mé go bhfuil tusa
Anocht ar bhuaic réime,
Iarraim féin ort aisce bheag:
Bí i do chara sa Chúirt Naofa
Ag gach file againn in Oilfinn
Nár tháinig fós i raon na geite,
Ní fearacht tusa
Ar gheit uile
Do sheal abhus.

And because I am certain
That, tonight, you stand in glory,
I ask you a small favor:
In the Holy Court above,
Be a friend to every poet in Ireland
Who is still to reach epiphany,[31]
Unlike you
Whose time below
Was all epiphany.

Mo Mhada Beag

(do Thomás agus do Charol)

Mada beag mo dhán
Is maith an sás cuardaigh é,
Cé nach fios domsa féin
Cén earra a bheidh ina bhéal
Nuair a fhillfidh ón gcuardach;
Ach geallaim go roinnfead leat
A dhath is a thuairisc.

My Little Dog

(*for Tomás and Carol*)

My poetry is a little dog,
Good for going hunting,
Although I never know myself
What he'll come back carrying;
But I promise to share with you
The tone and the tidings.

DÁNTA EILE / OTHER POEMS (uncollected, 1951–1979)

Machnamh an Duine Stoite

Caithimse sealta in éad
Leis an dream a d'fhás
I dtaithí áilleacht chathartha,
Eaglais, stua, is foirgneamh ard,
Is íomhá chloiche greanta,
Saothar na bpéintéir oilte
Inár ndánlann taiscthe
Is an dréacht téadbhinn ceoil
Thugann aoibhneas ard don aigne.

Ní bhainim as na nithe seo fós
Toisc ainchleachta, iomlán taithnimh:
Is iad na nithe príomháille léir
Is fuíoll na saíochta sinseartha
A roinn mo dhaoine liom ar a dteallach,
A shuigh i gcoróin ar mo chroí óighe,
Is mó is lón do m'anam.

Feasta, Samhain 1951

Reflections of an Uprooted Man

There are times I'm jealous
Of the crowd that grew up
Familiar with urban beauty,
Cathedral, arch, tall building,
Images finely carved in stone,
The work of learned painters
Kept on show in our gallery,
And the sweet-stringed music
Highly pleasing to the mind.

I still don't fully appreciate
These things I came to late:
All the primitive things
And the remains of ancient lore
My people shared by the fire
Crowned my untried heart,
And feed my soul much more.

Feasta, November 1951

Rabhadh Uamhain

Níor char file riamh an focal cóir,
Ná ógfhear dian a leannán rúin,
Mar charais féin an dúil chlochaí,
Gur rinne cloch de do chroí
Gur lioc do mheon ina cló,
Ó rug sí ort a barróg fhuar,
An ghin chrua sheasc sheang,
Do rogha ar an gcré chollaí.

Ba phaidir leat gach leac
A thoillfeadh ina teampall adhartha,
D'íbirt aimrid do Bhandia na Cloiche
Bhí do dhúil dhanartha sa saothar buile
A thógais ina comhair buinne ar bhuinne.

Ó lean do chorp do mheon ina hairchis
Is léir rian a caidrimh ort,
Is ó thréigis an chré ar an gcloch
Ní cuibhe duit a cuilt fút:
Seastar ar shúil an bhealaigh tú,
Mar rabhadh uamhain do chách.

Comhar, Meitheamh 1954

A Dire Warning

No poet ever loved the right word,
Or ardent young man his secret love,
As you loved the substance of stone—
So much you made a stone of your heart
And battered your nature into its shape,
Since it took you in its cold embrace,
That hard, sterile, flattened creation
Which you prefer to flesh and clay.

You made a prayer of every flagstone
Fit for building a temple of worship,
Your fruitless offering to the Stone Goddess,
As you coldly focused on the folly
You erected for her, layer by layer.

Since your body followed your mind after her,
The effect on you is plain to see,
And since you abandoned clay for stone,
A blanket of earth underneath you
Doesn't suit you anymore:
So stand instead in the middle of the road
As a dire warning to us all.

Comhar, June 1954

Trí Nithe

Trí nithe atá ar mo thí:
An bhroinn is an t-oileán i mo dhiaidh
Is an uaigh liom ag fanacht.

Ní fiach cothrom a bhfiachsan,
Triúr sa tóir ar dhuine amháin
Is ar chlár m'éadain a mbranda.

Mo bheanna a thabhairt liom
Ón mbroinn is ón oileán
Níor dhodhéanta leis an aimsir,

Ach níor bhua mo bhua fós
Is an uaigh ansiúd romham
A béal aici ar leathadh.

Agus, Meán Fómhair 1961

Three Things

Three things are closing in on me:
The womb and island at my back,
And the grave waiting for me.

The hunt is far from fair:
Three going after one,
And their seal upon my brow.

To come away unscathed
From the womb and the island
Was not impossible, with time,

But I'm still not home and dry,
With the grave there before me
And its mouth open wide.

Agus, September 1961

Do Mo Dhánta

Faighidís caidéis díbh
Na comharsain, más áil leo é,
Tá sibh gléasta agam,
Go feadh m'acmhainne féin,
Gan cabhair ó aon,
Is bíodh a fhios acu feasta
Nár tháinig ní gan cháim
Ach ó láimh Dé.

Cá bhfuil an t-aiteas
Trínar lingeadh sibh,
I gcéaduair ar an saol?
Is tá inchis bhur dtoirchithe
Imithe mar thinneas ó aréir,
Ach mo bheannacht in bhur dteannta
Ós mé bhur n-athair go léir.

Bhur máithreacha níor chaill libh
Ach silleadh súl nó sméid,
Meangadh gáire nó comhrá béil;
Duine acu níor iompair lá sibh
Ní áirím trí ráithe féin.

Dóchas, 1964

To My Poems

Neighbors can pass remarks
About you all they like,
But I have fitted you out
As best I can,
With help from no one;
And let them know from now
That perfection only comes
From the hand of God.

Where is the thrill
With which you leapt
At first into this life?
And the trouble over your delivery
Is like a forgotten illness;
But as I'm father to you all,
I bless you on your way.

Your mothers spared you no more
Than a glance or a nod,
A smile or passing word;
Not one of them carried you for a day,
Never mind three trimesters.

Dóchas, 1964

Strainséir

An mhaidin a raibh mo mháthair
á cur i gcré, i dtalamh,
chuaigh mé thart ar gach giodán
dár thaithigh mé i mo ghasúr,
gur fhágas slán ag cloch
ag móinín, ulán, céim, is carraig,
is chonac triúr ógfhear
faoi dhungaraí ar leoraí,
is mheasas gurbh amhlaidh
a bhí orthu fuireach calaidh,
is mheabhraíos féin go greannmhar
céard déarfadh m'athair mór fadó
dá bhfeiceadh roimhe an tsamhail;
ach leis sin rinne na fir
comharthaí lena lámha is beannú,
ach mheasas go raibh íoróin tríd an mbeannú,
go mba strainséir mé i mo dhúiche feasta
is go mba orm féin a bhí fuireach calaidh.

Cnuasach, 1966

Stranger

On the morning my mother was buried,
I went round every patch of land
I used to know when I was a boy,
Until I said goodbye to stone,
Bog-patch, boulder, ravine and rock,
And I saw three young men
In dungarees, upon a lorry,
And gauged that they were caught out
After a sudden turn in the weather,
And I remembered with amusement
What my granddad would have said
Had he encountered the sight before him;
But just then the men waved their arms
At me in greeting and bade hello,
Although I sensed an irony within
The greeting, and that I was a stranger
In my homeland for evermore,
Caught out after the weather had turned.

Cnuasach, 1966

Clochadóir

Chonaic mé clochadóir
In airde ar scafall
Is é ag tógail tí.
Chonaic fós é ag tomhais
Ag meá is ag brath na gcloch,
Is chonaic mé a liacht
Cloch is spalla a shín
Chuig a ghiolla anuas
Nuair nár thoill go beacht
Ina hionad cheart sa mbuinne nua:
Mise a bhéarfadh cuid mhór
Ar a bheith chomh deas chuig mo ghnó.

Dán-Phostaer

Stonemason

I saw a stonemason
High on a scaffold
Building a house.
I saw him measuring,
Feeling and weighing
The stones with his hands,
And saw how many
Stones and spalls
He would hand down
To his apprentice below
When they failed to fit
Into the right place
In the new row:
I would give a lot
To be as deft
At my handiwork.

A Poster-Poem

Eagla

Níor chuala tú féin ná do bhuíon
Scéala an tí mhóir thiar
Idir uille is glúin á aisnéis,
Is shuigh sibh síos gan chol
Os comhair na tine go sásta.

Bhí tú féin i do bhurla macnais
Ar an teallach in aice an fhíona,
Ach d'aird fós ar do ghnó
I lár na hoíche fuaire,
Tráth raibh díon an tí sin
Ag fógairt gála is gailige báistí.

Bhí m'aird féin ar an seantriath
Is ar a chaofach mná ar an mballa:
Iad beirt in dhá phortráid sáinnithe
Le trí chéad bliain is breis.

Ach mise a chuala an scéal
Idir uille is glúin á aisnéis
Bhuail eagla m'anama mé
Go dtabharfaidís bóthar dom is bata,
Is go mbeadh an chonairt le mo shála.

Carn, Earrach 1978

Fear

Neither you nor your tribe heard
The tale of the Big House in the West
Relayed between elbow and knee,
And so you sat before the fire
Readily and without a qualm.

You were a bundle of comfort and ease
There, beside the hearth and wine,
Though your wariness returned
In the middle of the chilly night,
When the roof of that same house
Drummed with gales and blasts of rain.

My mind was on the old lord
And his good lady on the wall.
Each one captured in a portrait
For three hundred years and more.

But having heard the story before,
Relayed between elbow and knee,
I was gripped with mortal fear
That I'd be shown the road, the stick,
And the bloodhounds chasing after me.

Carn, Spring 1978

from

BÉASA AN TÚIR

[The Ways[32] of the Tower]

(1984)

Amhras

Níor thug tú riamh cead
Don chéir leá i gceart
Ach ghabh tréith na cloiche,
Ionas nach eol dom anocht
An cloch chrua nó céir
Fírinne nó bréag thusa.

Doubt

You never allowed
The wax to melt properly
But hardened into stone,
So tonight I do not know
If hard stone or wax
Is the real you. Or not.

Sean-Mhicil

Nuair is fonn liom dul thar teorainn,
Nó céim a thabhairt thar chleacht,
Seasann Sean-Mhicil romham sa ród
Ag caitheamh seilí amach go fras
Is ag cangailt plug tobac.

É ag piocadh feamainne lena chrúba
Aníos as croí na duirlinge:
Seilí ag titim ar mhulláin bheaga,
Is gach seile ag glacadh a chló féin;
Micil ag caitheamh anuas ar lucht na huaire.

Tá tú ann fós a dhaigéid fir,
Ag cangailt is ag mungailt leat,
Is má d'imigh mise thar chleacht,
Ar scoitheas riamh do scáth im' ród?
Ar chuir focal as do stór ó chion?

Old Michael

When I feel like going beyond bounds
Or taking a step outside of custom,
Old Michael stands before me in the road,
Casting his spittle copiously down
And chewing plug tobacco.

Picking seaweed with his big hands
Up from the heart of the shore,
With spittle falling on the small round stones[33]
And every spittle forming its own shape:
Michael casting judgment on people nowadays.

You're still there, big man,
Champing and chewing away.
And if I went beyond custom,
Did I ever scatter your shadow on my way?
Or devalue one word from your store?

Tuige Duit a Theacht

(do Áine, i ndilchuimhne)

A chait dhuibh a thagann
Ar lic na fuinneoige,
Ag slíocadh an phána fhuair,
Tá tusa is mé féin
In éagmais an té
A riarfadh go fial orainn.

Tuige duit a theacht, a chait,
Ag súil le do chuid gach lá?
Níl agam duit ach cumha
Is ní dhéanfaimid béile de,
Is go mb'fhearr linn araon
É bheith faoi chónaí go buan.

Why Do You Come Here?

(for Áine, in loving memory)[34]

Black cat on the window sill,
Licking the cold pane of glass,
Both you and I miss the one
Who would always provide for us.

Cat, why do you come each day
Expecting your usual fare?
All that I have for you is loss,
And that won't feed anybody,
And you and I would both prefer
To let it rest, forever.

An tAsal Beag Dubh

Ar bhóthar an Spidéil
An lá ar nochtaíodh an leacht
I reilig an Bhóthair Mhóir,
Is clocha sneachta ag rince,
Cé d'fheicfinn cois claí
Is a thóin fós le gaoith,
Ach an t-asal beag dubh.
Céard a thug ann thú, a asail?
Ní fhaca mé sa reilig thú—
Arbh é nár ligeadh isteach thú?
Nach cuma, a asail bhig fáin,
Bhain tú geit as duine amháin.

The Little Black Donkey

The day that the gravestone
For Ó Conaire was unveiled
In Bohermore Cemetery,[35]
The hailstones were dancing,
And who did I see by a wall
But the little black donkey,
His backside still to the breeze.
What brought you there, donkey?
I didn't see you in the graveyard—
Did they refuse to let you in?
Never mind, little wanderer,
You gave one man a start, at least.

Do Eoghan Ó Tuairisc

A ridire ghil an phinn
A thug tairise don naonúr,
Is do bhé bhán an dáin
Faoi seach is le lán toil,
Táid ann a déarfadh gur thréigis
Ciall is maoin is fáltas,
Is fíor nár mhór do shuim
I gcruinniú stóir ná éadála
Ba leor leis an mbé bhán
Do chroí aici is t'anam.

Uaigneach thar meán ár saincheird;
Gnó aonarach gnó an dáin
Dá dtagann dua is duainéis
Guala gan bhráthair fear a dhéanta.

An fhad is mhaireas siolla,
Den fhriotal b'ansa leat féin
Mairfidh clú ort, is iomrá
Is mairfidh d'íomhá ghrámhar.
An déirc atá fanta ag do chairde;
Ach an dream nár char an briathar,
Is nár thuig do thoisc ná do mhian,
Ní mór ar fad an scéal iad.

B'ait leat teanga a chur
Go sprioc a cumais amach
Go nascfadh leis an uilíocht;
Ní cur as riocht a b'áil leat,
Óir ba mhór agat gradam teanga.

For Eoghan Ó Tuairisc

White knight of the pen
Who loyally served the Nine[36]
And the White Goddess of poetry,
Respectively and with all your will,
Some would say you abandoned
Common sense and self-interest,
And it's true you cared little
For garnering riches and gold;
Enough for the Goddess to own
Your very heart and soul.

Our craft is lonelier than most,
Poetry a solitary trade,
That gives rise to grief and bother
The poet must shoulder all alone.

As long as one syllable remains
Of the speech that you so loved,
Your name and reputation will last,
And so will your loving image—
A small consolation to your friends;
But those who don't appreciate the word,
Who didn't grasp your aim or ambition,
They're not worth bothering about.

You wanted to extend language
As far as it could reach,[37]
To connect with the universal,
Not to mangle or misshape it,
Since language was so dear to you.

A chara ionúin ghrámhair
Nach raibh fáthadh an gháire
Ariamh i bhfad as do shúil
Ná as cúinne do bhéil,
Is fada uainn anocht do ghnúis;
Gnúis Dé nára fada uait féin.

My loving and beloved friend,
With a smile never far from your eyes
Or from the corner of your mouth,
Tonight your face is far from us;
May God's face not be far from you.

Aiféala

Bhéarfainn mo bhoige ar chruas,
Bhéarfainn mo shéimhe ar ghairbhe,
Is bheirim fós mo mhíle mallacht,
Do chloch, do charraig, is do chladach,
Nár chuir an sioc im' chnámha,
Nuair a bhí acu é a dhéanamh.

Regret

I'd give my softness for toughness,
I'd give my mildness for roughness,
And I give a thousand curses
To shore and rock and stone
For not putting ice into my bones
When they could have done.

Bród

Luigh ar do chranna foirtil
Má tá siad fós le fáil,
Is nach bhfuilid mar mheasaim,
Snoite is caite go cnámh:
Nuair nár tháinig chugat an ní
Nach dtagann roimh aois
Ná le haois féin ag an té
Ar ar leag an bhé bhán
Go trom anuas a lámh,
Mholfainn duit, a ghasúir,
Luí ar do bhród cé fuar.

Pride

Lean on your own stout oars
If they are still around,
And not, as I suspect,
Worn down to the bone:
Since it didn't come to you,
That which only comes with age,
And not even with age
To the one on whom the Muse
Has firmly laid her hand,
Then I advise you, boy,
Lean on your pride however cold.

Folamh

Geallaim duit nach ort an locht
Má tá mála an tsnáth ghil
Folamh id' pháirt anocht.
Oíche dhuairc gheimhridh
A bheadh ann i lár an tsamhraidh,
Ach snáth an charadais eadrainn
A bheith gearrtha ón dúid anuas.
Tusa a rinne samhradh dom
Fad a mhair an snáth,
An sníomhfar a chomh-mhaith go brách?

Empty

I swear it's not your fault
If the purse for the bright thread
Is empty, on your side, tonight.
It would be a dark winter night
In the middle of summer
If the thread of friendship between us
Was cut right down to the end.
You who made it summer for me
As long as the thread held out,
Will you ever spin another as good?

from

CRAOBHÓG DÁN

[A Sprig of Poems]

(1986)[38]

Solas

Chaithfeadh mo cholainn cloigeann eile
Is níor mhiste ar mo theach dhá dhoras.
Ariamh níor dhiúltaigh solas
Ó na ceithre hairde nuair tháinig;
Ach iarraim ar an solas iasachta
Gan mo sholas féin a mhúchadh.

Light

My body could use another head
And my house could do with two doors.
For I never rejected light
From anywhere when it came;
But I ask the foreign light
Not to drown out my own.

Beir ar Do Pheann

A mhanaigh, beir ar do pheann
Is lean go dlúth a ndeirim,
Ach ná sceith do neach mo rún
Go stada an bás do thochras
Is fág do scríbhinn ansin
Ar bhalla fuar do chillín.

Take Up Your Pen

Monk, take up your pen
And follow closely what I say,
But don't let anyone in on my secret
Till death stops your yarn-spinning,
And leave your writing there
On the cold wall of your cell.

Bail is Beannú

"Bail is beannú
Is rathúnas Dé ort,"
A deiridís seanmhná liom
Le linn dóibh
A bheith ag caitheamh
Seilí ar mo bhaithis.
Is maith an seans
Gur beannacht i dteanga eile
A chaithfear liom feasta
Is mholfainn dom féin
Gan comhrá a spreagadh
Ar eagla go labhródh
Clocha glasa ar na creaga
Is go siúlfainn ar mo chroí
Le hualach cantail.

Benediction (i)

"May God bless, protect and be good to you,"
The old women said when I was a boy,
Casting their spittle on the crown of my head.
Chances are that any blessing cast
My way now will be in another tongue;
And so I warn myself not to strike up
A conversation in case the crag's grey rocks
Talk back and I tread on my heart in frustration.

Benediction (ii)

"God bless, protect and be good to you,"
The old women used to say,
Spitting on my crown for luck.
From now on, it's more likely
That any blessing cast my way
Will be in a different language.
And I say to myself in warning,
"Don't strike up a conversation
For fear the grey stones on the crags
Answer you back and you tread
On your heart in frustration."

Gráinne Eile Fós

Gur mheall sí leannán
Ní mhionnóinn féin,
Go bhfuair deis suirí leis
Ní heol dom é,
Ach shaolaigh leanbh
Thíos faoin deic
Ina long féin!
Sos ní raibh aici
An uair sin féin,
Ó cuireadh fios uirthi
Teacht ar bord
Le cath a thabhairt do Thurcaigh:
Scaip sí an namhaid
Soir is siar
Is theith lena anam an Turcach:
"Tabhair leat an méid sin," ar sise
"Ó lámha neamhchoisricthe."
Uair eile is cath ar siúl,
Thug faoi deara a mac féin
A bheith ag dul i bhfolach
Taobh a tóna;
Ní bog a bhí sí ach searbh:
"B'éigean duit a dhul ag caitheamh
Ón áit ar tháinig tú as."
Misneach uile mná ár dtíre
Ach ar ghualainn Ghráinne an Iarthair
Ní raibh i nGráinne Fhinn
Ach áilleagán mná is peata;
Samhail Mháire Rua í Gráinne Ní Mháille
Nó b'fhéidir Méabh Chruachan.

The Greatest Gráinne of Them All[39]

That she seduced some lover—
I couldn't swear to it;
And had her way with him—
It's not for me to know,
But a child was born
Below deck
On her own ship.
Even then, she didn't rest:
Called back on board
To fight the Turks,[40]
She scattered the enemy
East and west
Till the Turk fled for his life:
"Take that," she said,
"From unblessed hands."
Another time in the heat of battle,
She caught her own son
Hiding behind her bum,
And didn't mince her words:
"So you had to go back
Where you came from!"
Our country's women
Are made of courage,
But next to Gráinne Mhaol,
Finn McCool's Gráinne
Is a dolly bird, a pet;
Our "Grace-of-the-West"
Is more akin to Red Mary[41]
or else, perhaps, Medbh
of Croghan, Queen of Connacht.[42]

NOTES TO INTRODUCTION

1. A phrase adapted from Máirtín Ó Direáin, "Bile a Thit" ["Integrity"], *Na Dánta* (Indreabhán: Cló Iar-Chonnacht, 2010), 220.
2. Ó Direáin, "Ionracas," *Na Dánta*, 114.
3. Areas of Ireland in which English is the majority language.
4. Ó Direáin, "Deireadh Ré" ["End of an Era"], *Na Dánta*, 93.
5. Ó Direáin, "Deireadh Oileáin" ["End of an Island"] and "Bua na Mara" ["The Sea's Victory"], *Na Dánta*, 104 and 92, respectively.
6. Ó Direáin, "Strainséir" ["Stranger"], *Na Dánta*, 262.
7. "Ach ó thosaigh na clocha glasa / Ag dul i gcruth brionglóide i m'aigne [...]." Ó Direáin, "Berkeley," *Na Dánta*, 170.
8. Heaney, "Mint," *Opened Ground: Poems 1966–1996* (London: Faber and Faber, 1998), 396.
9. Ó Direáin chose his phrase "oileán rún" to consciously play on the ambiguity of the word "rún" which can mean "beloved" and also "secret."
10. From "Neamhionraic Gach Beo" ["No Integrity among the Living"], *Na Dánta*, 239.
11. Louis MacNeice's description of the "world" in his seminal poem "Snow." MacNeice, *Collected Poems*, ed. E. R. Dodds (London: Faber and Faber, 1979), 30.
12. See Ó Direáin, "Do Easnamh" ["Something Missing"], *Na Dánta*, 165.
13. See, for example, Ó Direáin, "Cuimhní" ["Memories"] and "Cuimhní Nollag" ["Christmas Memories"], *Na Dánta*, 36 and 64, respectively.
14. Especially the early poems: see, for example, Ó Direáin, "Tnúth" ["Longing"], *Na Dánta*, 46.
15. Ó Direáin, "Ath-Bheatrice" ["Another Beatrice"], *Na Dánta*, 293.
16. Ó Direáin, "Do Mhnaoi nach Luaifead" ["To X"], *Na Dánta*, 25.
17. Ó Direáin, "Caoin Tú Féin, a Bhean" ["Cry for Yourself, Woman"], *Na Dánta*, 96.
18. Alexander Pushkin, "I Loved You," in *Pushkin Threefold: Narrative, Lyric, Polemic, and Ribald Verse*, ed. and trans. Walter Arndt (New York: Dutton, 1972).
19. Ó Direáin, "Ár gCuid dá Chéile" ["Our Share of Each Other"], *Na Dánta*, 105.
20. Ó Direáin, *Na Dánta*, 153. See also "Leag Uait na hAirm" ["Lay Down Your Arms"], *Na Dánta*, 168; and "Eala-Bhean" ["Swan-Woman"], *Na Dánta*, 189.
21. Ó Direáin, "Caoin Tú Féin, a Bhean," *Na Dánta*, 96. In a later poem, "Cor sa Leamhnacht," men (including the poet himself) are presented as just as susceptible to being led astray: *Na Dánta*, 243.

22. "Do Phegg Monahan" ["For Pegg Monahan"], *Na Dánta*, 91.
23. "Do Mháire Nic Giolla Mhártain," *Na Dánta*, 94.
24. From "Coinnle Ar Lasadh" ["Candles Glowing"] to "Brón Mo Mháthar" ["My Mother's Grief"], "Mo Mháthair" ["My Mother"] and beyond. See *Na Dánta*, 23, 99, and 109, respectively.
25. Ó Direáin, *Na Dánta*, 211 and 288, respectively.
26. Ó Direáin, *Na Dánta*, 204 and 290, respectively.
27. Nuala Ní Dhomhnaill, "Why I Choose to Write in Irish, the Corpse that Sits Up and Talks Back," in Ní Dhomhnaill, *Selected Essays*, ed. Oona Frawley (Dublin: New Island, 2005), 10–24 (p. 11).
28. The collection Ár *Ré Dhearóil* was published in 1962.
29. Ó Direáin, *Na Dánta*, 121.
30. The Black and Tans and the Auxiliaries.
31. For example, "Coinnle ar Lasadh" ["Candles Lit"], *Na Dánta*, 23.
32. Excerpt from "Gráinne Eile Fós" ["The Greatest Gráinne of Them All"], the final poem in Ó Direáin's collection *Craobhóg Dán* (1986), published just two years before his death: *Na Dánta*, 321.
33. Gráinne Ní Mháille (c. 1530–1603?), also known as Gráinne Mhaol and Grace O'Malley.
34. Máire Rua MacMahon, "Lady of Lemaneagh" (1615/16–1686).
35. Ó Direáin, *Na Dánta*, 146.
36. Ó Direáin, *Na Dánta*, 70: "carnán trodán / Faoi ualach deannaigh / Inár ndiaidh in Oifig Stáit." The abbreviation (Govt.) in the translation is intended to be as ugly as the dusty pile of files (and probably the word "Stáit") is to the poet.
37. Ó Direáin, *Na Dánta*, 91.
38. Ó Direáin, "Dom Féin" ["To Myself"], *Na Dánta*, 142.
39. The state of the nation is yet another theme for Ó Direáin.
40. See, for example, "Eochair na Foghlama" ["The Key to Learning"], *Na Dánta*, 212; "Do Mo Dhánta" ["To My Poems"], 261 and "Clochadóir" ["Stonemason"], 266.
41. See, for example, Ó Direáin, "Maidin Domhnaigh" ["Sunday Morning"], *Na Dánta*, 63 and "Rún na mBan" ["The Women's Secret"], 66.
42. Ó Direáin, "Sólás na Ceirde" ["The Solace of Art"], *Na Dánta*, 202.
43. Ó Direáin, "Ualach" ["Burden"], *Na Dánta*, 201. Note that Ó Direáin placed these two poems side by side, Janus-like: in the first, the art or craft of poetry is a "burden"; and in the second, it is presented as a "solace."
44. Ó Direáin, "Machnamh an Mharcaigh" ["The Rider's Thought"] and "Mo Cheirdse" ["My Craft"]: *Na Dánta*, 219 and 181, respectively.

45. The national Irish-language theatre of Ireland.
46. See, for example, "O'Casey" and "Don Ollamh Dáithí Ó hUaithne, R.I.P.", *Na Dánta*, 180 and 292, respectively.
47. Ó Direáin, "Mo Mhada Beag" ["My Little Dog"], *Na Dánta*, 244.
48. Frank Sewell, *Modern Irish Poetry: A New Alhambra* (Oxford: Oxford University Press, 2001), ch. 3.
49. Ó Direáin, "Dúshlán" ["Defiance"], *Na Dánta*, 153.
50. See, for example, "Réim na bhFaoileán" ["A Colony of Gulls"], *Na Dánta*, 162.
51. Literally, "a giant [of a] poet," referring mainly to Ó Direáin's stature in modern Irish-language poetry but also, in part, to his physical stature. See also Declan Collinge, "Ó Direáin: A Craggy Giant of Aran and a Giant of Irish Language Poetry," *Sunday Independent* (Ireland), March 11, 2018.
52. Ó Direáin, *Na Dánta*, 312.
53. See Ó Direáin's essay "Mise agus an Fhilíocht" ["Poetry and Me"], *Na Dánta*, 323–6 (p. 324).
54. Heaney, "Learning from Eliot," *Agenda* 27 (1989): 17–31.
55. See Cathal Ó Searcaigh, "An Fuascailteoir" ["The Liberator"], *An Bealach 'na Bhaile: Homecoming* (Indreabhán: Cló Iar-Chonnacht, 1993), 186; and Ó Direáin, "Mise agus an Fhilíocht," 325.
56. Ó Direáin, "Ár Ré Dhearóil" ["Our Wretched Era"], *Na Dánta*, 129.
57. Ó Direáin, "Cúis Uamhain" ["A Cause for Dread"], *Na Dánta*, 173.
58. Ó Direáin, *Na Dánta*, 148.
59. Collinge, "Ó Direáin: A Craggy Giant of Aran and a Giant of Irish Language Poetry."
60. MacNeice, "An Eclogue for Christmas," *Collected Poems*, 35.
61. Ó Direáin, "Machnamh an Duine Stoite" ["Reflections of an Uprooted Man"], *Na Dánta*, 251.
62. Dublin: An Clóchomhar, 1980.
63. Ó Direáin, "Ó Mórna," *Na Dánta*, 79–83.
64. Ó Direáin, "Comhchríoch" ["Winding Up the Same Way"], *Na Dánta*, 168.
65. Andrew Marvell, "To His Coy Mistress" (1681).
66. See, for example, "Do Thonn Bheag" ["To a Tiny Wave"], *Na Dánta*, 29.
67. See "Cúirt ar Dhán" ["Poem in the Dock"], *Na Dánta*, 231.
68. Hank Williams, "I'll Never Get Out of This World Alive," *The Best of Hank Williams* (Spectrum Music, 1998).
69. See Ó Direáin, "Trí Gháire" ["Three Laughs"], *Na Dánta*, 240; and "Mo Mháthair," 109.

70. See Ó Direáin, "Séamus Ó Conghaile" ["James Connolly"], "An Stailc" ["The Strike"], "De Dheasca an Úis" ["Because of Usury"], "Éire ina bhfuil Romhainn" ["Ireland in the Time Left to Us"], *Na Dánta*, 33, 102, 117, and 155, respectively. Translations of all of these poems appear in an earlier (and highly recommended) bilingual selection of Ó Direáin's poems: *Máirtín Ó Direáin: Tacar Dánta / Selected Poems*, ed. Tomás Mac Síomóin and Douglas Sealy (Newbridge, Co. Kildare: Goldsmith Press, 1984, 1992).
71. Ó Direáin, "Sólás na Ceirde" ["The Solas of Art"], *Na Dánta*, 202.

BIBLIOGRAPHY

Collinge, Declan. "Ó Direáin: A Craggy Giant of Aran and a Giant of Irish Language Poetry." *Sunday Independent* (Ireland), March 11, 2018.

Heaney, Seamus. "Learning from Eliot." *Agenda* 27 (1989): 17–31.

———. *Opened Ground: Poems 1966–1996*. London: Faber and Faber, 1998.

Mac Giolla Léith, Caoimhín, ed. *Cime Mar Chách: Aistí ar Mháirtín Ó Direáin*. Dublin: Coiscéim, 1993.

MacNeice, Louis. *Collected Poems*. Edited by E. R. Dodds. London: Faber and Faber, 1979.

Marvell, Andrew. "To His Coy Mistress" (1681). <www.poetry foundation.org /poems/44688/to-his-coy-mistress>.

Ní Dhomhnaill, Nuala. *Selected Essays*. Edited by Oona Frawley. Dublin: New Island, 2005.

Ó Direáin, Máirtín. *Feamainn Bhealtaine*. Dublin: An Clóchomhar, 1961, 1971.

———. *Dánta 1939–1979*. Dublin: An Clóchomhar, 1980.

———. *Máirtín Ó Direáin: Tacar Dánta / Selected Poems*. Edited by Tomás Mac Síomóin and Douglas Sealy. Newbridge, Co. Kildare: Goldsmith Press, 1984, 1992.

———. *Na Dánta*. Indreabhán: Cló Iar-Chonnacht, 2010.

Ó hAnluain, Eoghan, ed. *Ón Ulán Ramhar Siar: Máirtín Ó Direáin ag Caint ar Chúlra Saoil Cuid dá Dhánta*. Dublin: An Clóchomhar, 2002.

Ó Searcaigh, Cathal. *An Bealach 'na Bhaile: Homecoming*. Indreabhán: Cló Iar-Chonnacht, 1993.

Pushkin, Alexander. *Pushkin Threefold: Narrative, Lyric, Polemic, and Ribald Verse*. Edited and translated by Walter Arndt. New York: Dutton, 1972.

Robinson, Tim. *Stones of Aran: Pilgrimage*, 3rd edn. London: Penguin, 1990.

Sewell, Frank. *Modern Irish Poetry: A New Alhambra*. Oxford: Oxford University Press, 2001.

Williams, Hank. *The Best of Hank Williams*. Spectrum Music, 1998.

NOTES TO POEMS

1. This poem is partly based on a certain James O'Flaherty whose cattle were driven over a cliff in 1881 during the Land War.
2. Pádraig Ó Concheanainn (c. 1907–88) grew up on the Aran Islands. A native Irish speaker, he became a teacher and married and settled in Dublin where he worked as a newsreader for the Irish-language news on Raidió Éireann. He served as secretary of publisher An Clóchomhar.
3. For information on this ancient structure (on the largest of the Aran Islands) and the "four" who gave it its name, see Tim Robinson, *Stones of Aran: Labyrinth* (New York: NYRB, 2009), 297–307.
4. This poem refers to the remains of St. Enda's monastery on Inis Mór. See Robinson, *Stones of Aran*, 66–73.
5. In order of appearance, the real place names listed in this poem have meanings or associative meanings which include or suggest "Ford of the Shallow" (or "of the Reef" or "Shingle"), "Glen of the Smoldering (or Burnt-Out) Things" (alternatively, Glen of the "Cut-off Pieces" or "Dark, Gloomy Places"), "Brae" (or "Hill"), the "Old Churchyard" (or "Old Cemetery"), "Cormac's Glen," and "The Dark Glen."
6. A reference to a review of Ó Direáin's work by Seán Ó Ríordáin whom the former viewed as a "brother" poet.
7. The "bag for the bright thread" is, according to Dinneen's Dictionary, "a choice place"; to be in that bag or purse is to be "restored to favor." See Muiris Mac Conghail, "Poet of the Bright Thread: The Poetry of Máirtín Ó Direáin," *Irish University Review* 18, no. 2 (Autumn 1988): 181–90. Ó Direáin's poems present "the bright thread" as a love token, preserved in a special bag or purse as long as the love itself lasted.
8. An allusion to the anonymous, ninth-century poem "Pangur Bán," which has been translated by W. H. Auden and Seamus Heaney, among others. The most skillful translation to date is by Paul Muldoon, in *The Finest Music: Early Irish Lyrics*, ed. Maurice Riordain (London: Faber and Faber, 2014).
9. References to Conn Cétchathach ("Conn of the Hundred Battles") and Eoghan Rua Ó Néill (Owen Roe O'Neill).
10. In the original poem Ó Direáin refers to Pádraig Mac Piarais (Patrick Pearse) and "na laochra" ("the heroes"), suggesting organizations such as the Irish Volunteers, the Irish Citizen Army, and the Irish Republican Army before and during the Irish War of Independence (1919–1921).

11. Philosopher and Church of Ireland bishop George Berkeley (1685–1753).
12. "I have never laid great store by poetic glory, and whether my songs are praised or blamed matters little to me. But lay a sword on my bier, for I have been a good soldier in the wars of human liberation." —Heinrich Heine
13. Idiomatic and earthy, this is a reference to Ireland no longer creatively or economically sustaining Sean O'Casey, at least by the time of his "exile." The poem, as a whole, is influenced by Ó Direáin's knowledge of O'Casey's life and career; and the last stanza, especially, seems to echo or allude to an earlier exile, James Joyce. In the latter's novel *A Portrait of the Artist as a Young Man*, Ireland is imaged, at one point, as "the old sow that eats her farrow."
14. Ó Direáin is playing on the various meanings of the word "breac" [trout] that, in Irish, can also mean "a prize" or "a catch."
15. As well as "result," Ó Direáin's word "toradh" may also mean "fruit," "product" or "yield."
16. Trans. "trees" and, metaphorically, "supports," "pillars," "champions."
17. A knitting and embroidery technique used, here, as a metaphor suggesting "nature will out." Ó Direáin's mother was a talented knitter and earned money for the family using such skills. See Mac Conghail, "Poet of the Bright Thread," 181.
18. Another ancestor from the poet's own home village, Sruthán, on Inis Mór.
19. Ó Direáin's first two volumes of poetry, published in 1942 and 1943, respectively.
20. A reference to Aogán Ó Rathaille's poem "Cabhair Ní Ghoirfead" ["I'll Not Ask for Help"]. See *Dánta Aodhagáin Uí Rathaille: The Poems of Egan O Rahilly*, ed. Patrick S. Dinneen and Tadhg O'Donoghue, second edition, revised and enlarged by Breandán Ó Buachalla (London: Irish Texts Society, 1911, 2004).
21. Caitlín Maude (1941–82) was a poet, writer, musician, *sean-nós* (unaccompanied) singer, actress, dramatist and Irish-language activist. With themes spanning relationships, spirituality (Christian and other), and politics, her works include the album *Caitlín* (Gael-Linn, 1975) and Ciarán Ó Coigligh (ed.), *Caitlín Maude: Dánta, Drámaíocht agus Prós* (2005).
22. Ó Direáin uses the word "bile" which also means "a tree," often a sacred tree and probably (befitting Ó Cadhain) an oak.
23. A socialist and republican, Máirtín Ó Cadhain was the foremost twentieth-century prose writer in Irish and also a trenchant activist on behalf of Irish speakers, Gaeltacht communities, and the Irish people as a whole.

24. Described as a "royal champion," Murchú (Murchad Mac Briain), was the son of King BrianBorú. Word that Murchú's banner fell at the Battle of Clontarf (April 23, 1014) was interpreted by Brian as an ill-omen for "the men of Erin" whose valor would be lost along with Murchú who died fighting in the battle.
25. The three references here are to key military defeats in the so-called "collapse" of the Gaelic order: the Battle of Kinsale 1601, the Battle of Aughrim or Eachroim an Áir (Aughrim of the Slaughter) 1691, and the Battle of Scarriffholis (Donegal) 1650.
26. The need to remain in the saddle, to avoid dismounting and to shun the stone are allusions to the legendary Oisín and to the sudden and dramatic onset of age and death that he experienced.
27. The translation was first published (with the poet's commentary) in the anthology *Rogha an Fhile: The Poet's Choice*, ed. Eoghan Ó Tuairisc (London: Goldsmith Press, 1974).
28. Russian, meaning "dear one" (addressed to a woman). Ó Direáin's original could be translated, more literally, as an address to a much-treasured "gift (or wonder) of a woman."
29. Ó Direáin's reference to the "integrity" of an "island" is a deliberate echo of his own earlier work (see pp. 86–7 of this volume) and also of parts III and IV of Seán Ó Ríordáin's poem "Oileán agus Oileán Eile" ["One Island and Another"]: see Ó Ríordáin, *Selected Poems*, ed. Frank Sewell (New Haven and London: Yale University Press, in association with Cló Iar-Chonnacht, 2014), 90–5. Influenced by mid-twentieth-century Christian theology and by Gerard Manley Hopkins, both poets expressed, at times, the view that a natural thing such as a bird, an island, a child, or a child's soul, for example, is "true" to itself; whereas adult (sinful) humans, through deceit, deviation, or possibly even deracination, may become "untrue" to their "true self," their soul, or "island." Thus the dead, such as the lord and lady in this poem, have one advantage over the living: they are no longer capable of being untrue to themselves or of any unworthy error or failing.
30. An allusion to Seán Ó Ríordáin's neologism "an pianfhoclóir" [the pain-dictionary] in Ó Ríordáin's poem "Na Fathaigh" ("The Giants"). See Ó Ríordáin, *Selected Poems*, 52.
31. In this poem, Ó Direáin uses some of Ó Ríordáin's key terms and concepts such as "geit" ["startlement" or "epiphany"], outlined by Ó Ríordáin in the preface to his first collection *Eireaball Spideoige* (1952). See "Afterword" (trans. John

Dillon), in Ó Ríordáin, *Selected Poems*, 231–42 (p. 233). See also Ó Ríordáin's description of himself as a disciple of James Joyce in his poem "Joyce," Ibid., 210.

32. Trans. "ways," "manners," "habits."
33. Ó Direáin's term "mulláin" (plural) is defined in Dinneen's dictionary as "round granite stones found in the Aran Islands, always resting on the small end (the islands are of limestone formation)." See Patrick S. Dinneen, *Foclóir Gaedhilge agus Béarla / An Irish-English Dictionary* (Dublin: Irish Texts Society, 1904), p. 469. Available at https://celt.ucc.ie/Dinneen1.pdf.
34. Áine Colivet whom Ó Direáin married on September 4, 1945. She died in 1976.
35. Ó Direáin unveiled the headstone added to the grave of Pádraic Ó Conaire in 1982. The event in Bohermore Cemetery, Galway, was part of the centenary celebrations of Ó Conaire's birth on February 28, 1882. One of Ó Conaire's most well-known stories is "M'Asal Beag Dubh" ["My Little Black Donkey"].
36. The Nine Muses.
37. Ó Direáin also defended Seán Ó Ríordáin on the same grounds given in this stanza. See Seán Ó Coileáin, *Seán Ó Ríordáin: Beatha agus Saothar* (Dublin: An Clóchomhar, 1982, 1985), 241, 250. Also available in English: Seán Ó Coileáin, *Seán Ó Ríordáin: Life and Work*, trans. Micheál Ó hAodha (An Spidéal: Cló Iar-Chonnacht, 2018).
38. This late-flowering and slim collection of mostly very short poems of one or two stanzas was published just two years before the poet's death at the age of seventy-seven. The collection indicates a dwindling of Ó Direáin's creative powers but still contains poems of interest, and it features his final word on some recurring themes.
39. The mighty Gráinne Ní Mháille (c. 1530–1603?), also known as Gráinne Mhaol and Grace O'Malley. See Theresa D. Murray, "Gráinne Mhaol, Pirate Queen of Connacht: Behind the Legend," *History Ireland* 13, no. 2 (March–April 2005), 16–20. Available at <www.jstor.org/stable/27725236>.
40. Algerian corsairs. Ibid.
41. Máire Rua MacMahon, "Lady of Lemaneagh" (1615/16–1686).
42. Medbh [Maeve] of *Táin Bó Cuailgne* [The Táin or Cattle Raid of Cooley]. See Ciaran Carson, *The Táin* (London: Penguin Classics, 2007).